A Handbook on How Prudential Common Sense Can Save the World from Imminent Collapse

Peter Anthony Achilles Redpath

En Route Books and Media, LLC
Saint Louis, MO

⊛ENROUTE
Make the time

En Route Books and Media, LLC
5705 Rhodes Avenue
St. Louis, MO 63109

Cover credit: Sebastian Mahfood
Copyright © 2024 Peter Anthony Achilles Redpath

ISBN-13: 979-8-88870-256-7
Library of Congress Control Number:
Available online at https://catalog.loc.gov

No part of this book may be reproduced, stored in a retrieval system, or transmitted in any form, or by any means, electronic, mechanical, photocopying, or otherwise, without the prior written permission of the author.

Table of Contents

Ch. 1: Editor's Introduction: Why Care about Metaphysics and Prudence and Ending the Separation between Philosophy and Science?... 1

Ch. 2: Mortimer J. Adler on Universal Principles of Education..... 65

Ch. 3: The Essential Connection between Commonsense Philosophy and Leadership Excellence... 77

Ch. 4: The Ideal of a University... 97

Ch. 5: Petrarch's Failed Project 117

Chapter 1[1]

Editor's Introduction: Why Care about Metaphysics and Prudence and Ending the Separation between Philosophy and Science?

Ever since the start of the twentieth century, and especially toward the rise and end of World War II, some Western intellectuals started to recognize that something was radically wrong with modern Western civilization and culture, that these appeared to be in their twilight years. Starting in the 1930s, these thinkers began to diagnose the problem in some detail. In doing so, in one way or another, they tended to arrive at the same conclusion: outside of the intellectual order of what, even today, Westerners call 'science' or 'physical science,' the West had largely lost its conviction that any truth or wisdom existed. Outside this narrow intellectual sphere, most Westerners had largely turned into skeptics and sophists.

While many contemporary Westerners tend to view the West's present decline as due to a loss of faith, these intellectuals disagree. They attributed this decay to a loss of *logos*, of reason, especially of wisdom and prudence in touch with sense reality and common sense.

---

[1] This volume is composed of amended, previously published and unpublished, articles of mine. I thank En Route Books & Media publisher, Sebastian Mahfood, for encouraging me collect these essays in one book so as to make them more easily accessible to readers who have been following my research over the past fifty years and more.

Belief has not been something in decline in the modern West, or world in general. It has existed, is, everywhere. Even 'science' is supposed to be simply one more 'belief system,' or 'feeling,' supposedly superior to other forms of belief or feeling because it is an 'Enlightened,' not a backward, 'religious belief system' or 'feeling.' The problem with the modern world is not that we believe in nothing. It is that we believe in everything except religion in touch with commonsense reality. We have lost our understanding of the range of reason and have largely turned into skeptics and sophists: *secularized fideists*.

Hence, the peculiar mental extremism that Westerners tend to exhibit. On the one hand, like all skeptics, we pretend to shy away from being judgmental. Since the whole of truth and wisdom supposedly reside in 'physical science,' and since all truth and wisdom essentially involve being judgmental, not making judgments outside the area of physical science is supposed to be a self-evident principle of the modern Western creed. Anyone who does not unquestioningly follow this creed is supposed to be, evidently, intellectually backward, not a true believer, a rube, unsophisticated, and (worst of all), *intolerant*. Within the modern West's Enlightened belief system, the only sin (except for the *Enlightened*) is for a person to behave inconsistently with his or her belief system: to be a hypocrite.

Of course, as skeptics, Westerners cannot, with any intellectual consistency, rationally justify making any of the above skeptical judgments. Skeptical judgment is an oxymoron. Skeptics are not supposed to be judgmental. Enlightened skeptics, however, do not worry about being logically consistent. They know *with absolute certainty* that all knowledge is a kind of belief. Hence, modern Western skeptics do what skeptics always do within this situation: they use sophistry to defend their hubristic and imperious intellectual claims.

Anyone familiar with Western intellectual history knows: (1) metaphysical principles and the moral and intellectual virtue of prudence found civilizations and that, based upon these principles, civilizations generate cultures of different kinds; and (2) once cultures lose their conviction about the truth of their founding principles of metaphysics and prudence, they decay from within. Hence, the existence of strong metaphysical and prudential commonsense convictions generates civilizations, and skepticism and doubt about them kill civilizations.

Realizing these truths about civilizational and cultural experience, some Western thinkers of the last century recognized that the West needed a renaissance of metaphysical and moral reason to bridge the gap between wisdom and science that appeared to be the root cause of the skeptical and sophistic mindset that, for centuries, has been causing the West progressively to rot from within. Unhappily, having spent most of their lives diagnosing the problem, these scholars did not have time to do what, with their help, I have tried to do in this collection of essays—write the full story they had sought to tell.

1. Some reasons why philosophical metaphysics is essential to the existence and nature of philosophy, science

For centuries after the development of modern physical 'science,' professional Western 'philosophers' largely avoided the study of metaphysics. As I will show in this book, a chief reason they did so was because, long before the modern age had come to be, the West had largely lost its understanding of the nature of philosophy and science, and the crucial role that metaphysics and the virtue of prudence (uncommon common sense) play in relation to the existence and nature of philosophy and science. As a result, currently metaphysics has largely become the 'Cinderella of the Sciences,' and the West has largely lost its understanding of the nature of philosophy and science.

If asked about the nature of metaphysics, many people today, including many professional intellectuals, *philosophers* falsely-so-called, would answer in a way that would identify the study with something akin to 'news from the spirit world.' If asked about the nature of philosophy and science, most contemporary 'philosophers' could not precisely explain the nature of either; and most 'scientists,' also falsely-so-called, would likely conflate science with mathematical physics, but could give no rational explanation for so doing.

From a practical standpoint, educationally and culturally for the contemporary world, and the West especially, the results of this neglect of real metaphysics and its essential connection to the virtue of prudence combined with a general lack of understanding of the relation of both to philosophy, science, have been devastating.

In ancient Greek and later medieval times, metaphysics had been largely equivalent to what professional 'philosophers' today call 'philosophy of science.' During the high points of ancient Greek culture and the high Middle Ages of Christendom, *prudential metaphysics (prudently practiced/commonsense metaphysics)* was viewed as *first philosophy*. It was recognized to be: (1) the only human discipline that existed capable of judging the nature, divisions, and methods of the different arts and sciences, and (2) the only human science that could rationally judge the other sciences *and rationally explain how they relate to each other and justify their existence in relationship to human life as a whole.*

In the architectonically-arranged hierarchy of classical science, *prudential metaphysics* tended to be viewed as the final cause of all the other arts and sciences—the one science that all the other sciences were ordered toward generating as the highest intellectual achievement of the human mind and chief explanation for the nature and existence of the arts and sciences, human culture, and civilization. One reason for this is that some influential ancients, like Aristotle, had recognized that the principles of *commonsense metaphysics* were common to all the arts and sciences, and that devoid of integrated arts and sciences no culture can exist. Because all the arts and sciences borrow and use these principles as their chief measures, criteria, of truth, in a way, metaphysics provided for classical philosophical antiquity, classical culture, the chief means for fulfilling the Delphic Oracle's admonition to every human being that the key to achieving science is to 'know thyself.'

By, in some way, containing all the knowing principles borrowed from it and used in all the arts sciences, classical metaphysics contained for the arts and sciences the means of self-knowledge, of rationally explaining to practitioners of each and every science the origin and rational justification behind the commonsense assumptions they used as their starting points for judging truth within their respective disciplines. By so doing, it rationally justified the claims of all the arts and sciences to be arts or sciences at all, and not to be simple matters of belief or arbitrary dogmatism.

In a way, as the final cause of all the other arts and sciences, some ancients, like Aristotle, had recognized that all the other arts and sciences were borrowing, analogously transferring to their own disciplines, principles, rules, for measuring truth that chiefly belong to metaphysics. As a result, strictly speaking, metaphysics alone was worthy of the name *philosophy* or *science*. Even though the science of metaphysics had not existed in a fully-developed form prior to the philosophies, sciences, of physics and mathematics, the terms 'philosophy,' 'science,' had been analogously transferred to other divisions of human knowing (in a way had been given to them on loan, inasmuch as these divisions of knowing maintained an essential connection to the gradually-emerging science of meta-physics).

For this reason, absent commonsense, philosophical metaphysics (prudently practiced, commonsense metaphysics) strictly speaking, no coherent philosophy of education can exist; and no rational means exists to explain how: (1) *arts and sciences can integrate with each other to produce a common culture or civilization; or* (2) *how any art or science can exist at all. In fact, absent essential connection to prudently practiced, or commonsense, philosophical metaphysics, as I will show beyond reasonable doubt in these essays, strictly speaking, no art or science can exist.*

What I say in the paragraph immediately above is so true that, within the twentieth century, the negative effects of the West's loss of understanding of the nature of metaphysics in relation to arts and sciences started to cause 'Philosophy Departments' at colleges and universities, especially those dealing with classical philosophy, to become largely gutted. As a result, other disciplines, philosophical mimics, generally referred to by the oxymoronic title 'social sciences' (oxymoronic because, by nature, they are not social or scientific) attempted to replace metaphysics as the queen of the sciences.

Since they could not fulfill this role, higher education became weakened to the point that many institutions of higher learning have had to close, or will have to close. And the cost of education in general has skyrocketed.

We cannot be wrong about the nature of science and expect not to suffer damage educationally, culturally, politically, and economically.

While, during the twentieth century, the hate-metaphysics attitude that had dominated the West for several centuries had started to abate somewhat, it had come too late to save many of the West's institutions of higher learning from their essential quest to self-destruct. Having lost with metaphysics what little sense of self-identity and common sense they had had, they could no longer even pretend intelligently to explain to others precisely what was their nature or chief aim.

During this time, some metaphysics texts appeared to try to stem the tide of Western educational and cultural decay, including ones written by students of St. Thomas Aquinas (b. 1224/25; d. 1274). Most, if not all, of these were composed specifically for use in academic programs. None was especially successful because none was able to show in adequate detail: (1) how commonsense philosophical metaphysics is crucial to understanding the nature, divisions, and methods of the classical and contemporary sciences; and (2) for solving the host of educational and cultural problems that we face today as necessary effects of the West's loss of understanding of the nature of philosophical metaphysics and the role it plays in transmitting common sense and human culture and civilization from one generation to the next.

I edit these essays in this volume, then, in part, to help reverse this trend: to provide a relatively short work in philosophical metaphysics that will serve as a philosophy of science that can show in an intelligible, general way, the nature, methods, and divisions of the sciences, how these arose historically, and why they are reasonable.

I also write it, however, as a Christian, Thomistic metaphysics, because I think that only this metaphysics has the intellectual resources to: (1) bridge the gap between ancient and contemporary culture so as to end the centuries-old separation between philosophy and science; and (2) thereby, help stem, and reverse, the tide of the West's loss of common sense and cultural and civilizational decline.

2. **How Descartes became the proximate, modern cause of the gradual separation of philosophy and science, science and wisdom**

From the end of Greek antiquity up until the start of the twentieth century, the terms 'philosophy' and 'science' were largely used synonymously. For this reason, when he wrote his classic work in physics, Sir Issac Newton (b. 1642; d. 1727) understood himself to be working as a scientist/philosopher. Hence, he entitled his groundbreaking book in physics, *Principia mathematica philosophiae natu-*

ralis (*The Mathematical Principles of Natural Philosophy*, not *Principia mathematica scientiae naturalis* [*The Mathematical Principles of Natural Science*]). Further evidence of the truth of the claim made in the first sentence of this paragraph above is that St. Thomas Aquinas, who is well-known to have been influenced by Aristotle (b. 384 BC; d. 323 BC) and neo-Platonism, used these terms synonymously. Noting the radical difference between St. Thomas's understanding of 'science' and the prevailing contemporary notion, Armand A. Maurer (r.i.p.) (b. 1915; d. 2008) remarks:

> Today, no one would think of equating philosophy and science, even though there is little agreement as to what the distinction between them is. Science in general is thought of as any reasoned knowledge that is universal and systematic. The ideal of scientific knowledge is an exact science such as mathematical physics, which uses precise mathematical calculations and a highly refined method involving experimentation, formation of hypotheses and their verification. Whatever philosophy may be, it obviously does not fit this description.[2]

The move in the West toward separating the two terms and have them designate different human activities came about gradually,

---

[2] This usage was common for St. Thomas Aquinas, for example; see Armand A. Maurer, "Introduction," in Armand A. Maurer (ed.), *The Division and Methods of the Sciences: Commentary on the* de Trinitate *of Boethius, Questions V and VI* (Toronto: Pontifical Institute of Mediaeval Studies, 3rd rev. ed., 1963), VIII–IX.

over centuries, and had its proximate root in the work of the person often honorifically called, 'The Father of Modern Philosophy': René Descartes (b. 1596; d. 1650). Descartes thought of himself as divinely elected to be the first true philosopher *and* scientist, as someone who had given birth to true philosophy after centuries of intellectual decadence in which, strictly speaking, philosophy, science, had not existed. Prior to him, he claimed no one had possessed *The Method* of science, philosophy, as a system of clear and distinct ideas whereby human beings could finally completely know truth and totally eradicate doubt from our minds.

Strictly speaking, as I have argued extensively in my book *Cartesian Nightmare: An Introduction to Transcendental Sophistry*, Descartes was no philosopher.[3] Like Italian renaissance humanists before him, strictly speaking, he was a rhetorician, or sophist.[4] His sophistic method consisted of an elaborate reduction of philosophy to systematic logic (a logical system of supposedly clear and distinct ideas) as a means of separating mathematics and physics from the influence of metaphysics and revealed theology, while, simultaneously, identifying mathematics and physics with the whole of science, understood as rational, logically-systematic, knowledge of sense reality.

---

[3] For a detailed defense of this claim, see Peter A. Redpath, *Cartesian Nightmare: An Introduction to Transcendental Sophistry* (Amsterdam and Atlanta: Editions Rodopi, B.V., 1997).

[4] Regarding the conflation of humanism with rhetoric and poetry during the Italian renaissance, see Paul Oskar Kristeller, *Renaissance Thought: The Classic, Scholastic, and Humanist Strains* (New York: Harper & Row, Publishers, 1961).

As I show in the above-mentioned work, among the many mistakes Descartes made in working out his project were to: (1) conflate truth, science, and wisdom; (2) relocate truth, science, and wisdom from acts of intellect, or reason, to that of will; (3) replace the human soul with a 'mind,' which he confounded with a collection of ideas; and (4) separate philosophy, science, and wisdom from any essential connection to a human faculty, habit, or virtue whose first principle is the intellectual soul of an individually-existing human being, a soul/body composite.

For Descartes, to know, to possess truth, is identical with knowing scientifically. As Étienne Gilson (b. 1884; d. 1978) tells us, Descartes's grand project consisted in knowing everything by one method with the same amount of certainty or knowing nothing at all.[5] Descartes had reduced truth, all knowledge (including wisdom) to science and was condemned to possess the whole of science or no truth at all.

Further complicating his mistakes, Descartes reduced truth (and with it philosophy, science, and wisdom) to strength of will. According to him, truth is chiefly a relation between the human will and intellect, an act of will on the intellect, not of reason or intellect considered as such. For him, the power of the will to cause reason to attend to, or focus on, an idea, is the cause of all truth, is truth, just as weakness of will that causes reason (which is simply a collection of ideas) to wander under the influence of unrestrained imagination (again, simply a collection of ideas) is the cause of all error, is error.

---

[5] Étienne Gilson, *Unity of Philosophical Experience* (New York: Charles Scribner's Sons, 1965), 140.

By replacing the human soul with a collection of ideas he called a "mind" and eliminating from the individual knower any numerically-one and intrinsic principle, starting point, that generated many natural and acquired psychological powers, Descartes and his intellectual descendants became totally incapable of explaining how science, philosophy, can consist of many acts performed by numerically-one subject. In so doing, he: (1) separated wisdom, science, philosophy, from the individual intellect of the individual knower; (2) transformed wisdom, science, philosophy, into will-power having no individual as its principle of origin; and (3) changed the formal object of wisdom, science, philosophy into a system, or nominalistic collection of ideas or facts (somewhat resembling Plato's 'World of Forms'), clearly visible only to someone (like him) with a will supposedly strong enough to enable his mind to see it.

Regarding the physical world around us, Descartes maintained that only mathematical ideas viewed by an exceptionally strong will can stabilize reason to be able to apprehend truth about physical reality. Hence, long before Friedrich Nietzsche (b. 1884; d. 1900), in his founding principles, Descartes had made the egregious mistakes of alienating truth, philosophy, science, and wisdom from natural reason, human habituation, and intellectual virtue, and identifying all wisdom, science, and philosophy, including that about the physical universe, with practical science and practical science with will-power.

3. **How, by reducing metaphysics to history, Rousseau and his progeny replaced metaphysics with modern utopian socialism and transformed Cartesian will-power into the utopian socialist will-to-power**

Unhappily, in short, for subsequent generations, modern 'philosophy's' 'science's,' birth with Descartes had been accompanied by, founded upon: (1) a disordered understanding of the human person as a pure spirit: (2) an imperious, rationally-unjustifiable, attempt to reduce the whole of wisdom, philosophy, science, truth, and knowledge to some blind urge to power; and (3) a similar attempt to reduce all knowledge of the physical world around us to the order of modern mathematical physics (often today called 'empirical science' or 'positivism') and its method of productive reason. As a result, even if philosophy, science, had existed prior to him, anyone coming after him who accepted his method and imitated it, could not, strictly speaking, be a philosopher, scientist.

All of us are born into problems and difficulties we inherit from others. For centuries the Western world has been beset by a host of social problems that resulted from mistakes made over the last several centuries by Descartes and those who accepted many of the founding principles of their 'philosophies,' 'science,' upon disordered notions, first principles, of human nature, human knowing, and metaphysics that they, more or less, directly inherited from Descartes.

Consider some simple examples of such disordered ways of thinking common to the contemporary Western mind. Today, virtually all, somewhat-educated, Westerners tend unquestioningly to accept as self-evident truths that 'science' and 'positivistic science,' or 'mathematical physics,' are identical. Ask virtually any Western college student today the question, "What is truth?" and the student will tend to reply: "A fact," or "What is factual." Follow with the question, "What is a fact?", and the same student will tend to answer, "What can be proven." Ask, "What does the word 'proof' mean?", and the student will tend to say: "What can be scientifically, or experimentally, tested or demonstrated."

Among other things, evident about such replies is the tendency that contemporary Western college students have to rule out evident truths and many traditional subjects of scientific study (like metaphysics, ethics, politics) from possessing truth. The mind of the contemporary Western college student tends to reduce the whole of truth to positivism: the practical science of mathematical physics. Apart from accepting truth to exist in positivistic science, the contemporary Western college student, like most Western adults, tends to be an absolute skeptic.

This situation has become so pronounced in the contemporary West that, on 22 March 2011, the Vatican issued the declaration entitled *Decree on the Reform of Ecclesiastical Studies of Philosophy* regarding the crucial role of philosophy, especially metaphysics, in training priests. Commenting upon this declaration, Vatican Secretary of Education Cardinal Zenon Grocholewski said that the most fundamental aspects of life are under assault today: "[R]eason itself is menaced by utilitarianism, skepticism, relativism, and distrust of reason's ability to know the truth regarding the fundamental problems of life." He added that science and technology, those icons of what he called "materialist philosophies," cannot "satiate man's thirst in regard to the ultimate questions: What does happiness consist of? Who am I? Is the world the fruit of chance? What is my destiny? etc. Today, more than ever, the sciences are in need of wisdom."[6]

Westerners today owe the tendency to think precisely the way we now do about science and philosophy chiefly to another Frenchman: Jean-Jacques Rousseau (b. 1712; d. 1778). Like many thinkers of his time, Rousseau admired the twofold attempt by Descartes to overcome the growing skepticism of his age and, simultaneously, to separate philosophy and science from the influence of theology and theologians. Like other admirers of parts of Descartes's project, Rousseau recognized that Descartes's attempt metaphysically to refound science and philosophy in terms of a system of clear and distinct ideas was overly ambitious. He realized that the success of Descartes's dream to join all our ideas into a unified scientific body of knowledge depended upon overcoming a chief weakness in Descartes's system: the ability of substances to communicate.

As is well known, Descartes had attempted metaphysically to construct his scientific system by maintaining that only two substances exist, mind and matter; and that these substances cannot communicate. Descartes considered matter to be totally inactive and mind, or spirit, to be the only thing that acts.

Rousseau recognized that, in the real world, matter and mind communicate. Since Descartes could not explain this communication between the substances of mind, or spirit, and matter, Rousseau

---

[6] *Decree on the Reform of Ecclesiastical Studies of Philosophy* https://www.vatican.va/roman_curia/congregations/ccatheduc/documents/rc_con_ccatheduc_doc_20110128_dec-rif-filosofia_en.html.

resigned to overcome this failure by accepting a position that Descartes had rejected. He declared modern philosophy's principles to be *essentially dualistic, animistic, and obscure.*[7] Hence, Rousseau maintained, *only spirits are substances.* He thought that *only spirits exist and even apparently inanimate beings, like stones, are animate.*[8]

While Rousseau accepted Descartes's claim that science is a system of clear and distinct ideas, he rejected Descartes's contention that God had given us this system simultaneously whole in a multitude of clear and distinct ideas buried in our mind waiting there to be uncovered. Instead, Rousseau constructed an elaborate fairy tale: *a utopian history about human nature and origin that replaced metaphysics with history as the means to explain the nature and development of true science, philosophy.*

Rousseau maintained that, under the influence of the "voice of conscience," or "tolerance," God has intended this system of science, metaphysics, to emerge from the history of the human race through progressive self-development (what Westerners, today, tend to call "progress"). In this process, in his classic work entitled *Émile or On Education*, Rousseau claimed that God intends humanity's true teacher to be a person of inspired, or Enlightened, faith, the singular person of strong feeling who has only nature as a teacher.[8]

---

[7] Peter A. Redpath, *Masquerade of the Dream Walkers: Prophetic Theology from the Cartesians to Hegel* (Amsterdam and Atlanta: Editions Rodopi, B.V., 1998), 91–92; see, also, Jean-Jacques Rousseau, *Émile or On Education*, trans. Allan Bloom (New York: Basic Books, Inc., Publishers, 1979), 273–275 and 285–287.

[8] Redpath, *Masquerade of the Dream Walkers: Prophetic Theology from the Cartesians to Hegel*, 72.

Shortly prior to Rousseau, Newton had also rejected Descartes's metaphysical understanding of science as a system of clear and distinct ideas buried in his soul and had conceived of science, philosophy, metaphysics, as a prophetic history. Newton had conceived of this history to be deflated theology, historical truth about God's operation in creation.[9]

Metaphysically, historically, considered, Newton looked upon the whole universe and its parts as a riddle, a secret, that he could read by applying pure thought to the world around him, "certain mythic clues which God had left about the world to allow a sort of philosopher's treasure hunt to the esoteric brotherhood." He believed that a secret brotherhood had transmitted these truths, this hidden teaching, about the nature of universe in an unbroken chain back to the original cryptic revelation in Babylonia.[10]

Beyond these strange ideas, Newton thought that, "throughout history, God continuously raised up prophets to lead his people back to the original truth revealed to the first followers of Jesus." He believed he was one of these prophets, a magi "descended from a long line of scientific prophets who had anticipated his discoveries in a prefigured and oracular fashion." Apparently, he saw his birth on 25 December 1642 as a sign of his special relation to the Magi.

---

[9] Redpath, *Masquerade of the Dream Walkers: Prophetic Theology from the Cartesians to Hegel*, 15–16; see, also, Frank E. Manuel, *Isaac Newton, Historian* (Cambridge, Mass.: Harvard University Press, 1979), 89–121, 139–168.

[10] John Maynard Keynes, "Newton the Man," in Bernard Cohen and Richard S. Westfall (eds.), *Newton*, (New York and London, England: W. W. Norton and Company, Inc., 1995), 315.

In a fashion analogous to many Renaissance humanists and to the medieval Islamic thinker Averroes (ibn Rushd, b. 1126; d. 1198), Newton believed that Scripture hides a true teaching, philosophy, science, metaphysics. But, according to Newton, this teaching is about the history of creation, the original Christian religion, not a *mystical and esoteric* moral or metaphysical system (as many Renaissance humanists had thought) or a historically-emerging social system (as Rousseau had thought). In standard Renaissance humanist fashion, Newton maintained that the educational deficiency of their audience had caused Moses and other Biblical authors to describe this creation history poetically to make it comprehensible. By so doing, these writers gave to these simple truths about the original Christian religion and physical creation a lofty moral and metaphysical appearance that a correct exegesis of Scripture would deflate.[11]

In *Cartesian Nightmare* I have argued extensively that, despite claims by Gilson to the contrary, precisely speaking, Descartes did not move the West from the skepticism of Michel de Montaigne to a new philosophy. Precisely speaking, Descartes moved the West from the predominance of one branch of the classical liberal arts, the *trivium* (the poetry and rhetoric of Italian renaissance humanism) to another, the *quadrivium*.[12]

Strictly speaking, Descartes did not generate a new philosophy or a return to constructive philosophical thinking. He wedded to-

---

[11] Redpath, Redpath, *Masquerade of the Dream Walkers: Prophetic Theology from the Cartesians to Hegel*, 14–32.

[12] Redpath, *Cartesian Nightmare*, 20.

gether a new rhetoric and poetic view of the world in which mathematical abstraction united to a new logic of invention, not the rhetoric and poetic view of the world that had dominated Italian renaissance humanism, would prevail as the primary means by which Westerners would, from that point on, read the Book of Nature.[13]

In doing this, I maintain that Descartes: (1) was doing little more than making an attempted correction in the more major political revolution initiated centuries before him by Francesco Petrarcha (Petrarch, b. 1304; d. 1374) and (2), under the rubric of the *quadrivium*, was involving himself in a poetic and rhetorical continuation of the age-old battle between poets and philosophers that Plato (b. 424/423 BC; d. 348/347 BC) had described in Book Ten of his famous *Republic*. Under the rubric of the "Battle of the Arts" this conflict had resurfaced during the twelfth century between faculty members of the cathedral school of Chartres and the monastery of St. Victor in Paris; in the thirteenth century between members of the faculties of arts and theology at the University of Paris; and during the Italian renaissance with Petrarch and his Renaissance humanist followers.[14]

---

[13] Redpath, *Cartesian Nightmare*, 20.; see Gilson, *Unity of Philosophical Experience*, 125–126; for the groundbreaking work that shows how some medieval and renaissance humanists transformed the physical universe into a book and philosophy into a skill of reading that book, see Gerald Galgan, *The Logic of Modernity* (New York and London, New York University Press, 1982).

[14] Étienne Gilson, *History of Christian Philosophy in the Middle Ages* (New York: Random House, 7th printing, 1955), 314–323.

Part of the thesis of this introductory chapter is that we get a more accurate understanding of Descartes's scientific project and its affect upon subsequent generations if we see it as a continuation of the Italian renaissance humanist movement, if we see Descartes and his progeny not as coming out of, or continuing, the Western philosophical tradition (which had died centuries before Descartes), but as coming out of and continuing the Italian renaissance humanist (poetic/rhetorical) tradition.

Once we do this, we become better able to understand the modern and contemporary ages as a whole and to recognize the truth of a startling statement that Gilson makes in his classic, *Reason and Revelation in the Middle Ages*. There he tells any historian who might investigate the sources of "modern rationalism" that an uninterrupted chain of influence exists from the Averroistic tradition of the Master of Arts of Paris to the European freethinkers of the seventeenth and eighteenth centuries.[15]

Clearly, this neo-Averroistic tendency is present within much of the Italian, and post-Italian, renaissance humanist movement. It is clearly present later in Newton. I maintain that it is equally present in Descartes's metaphysical claim that philosophy, or science, is a hidden system buried in his soul like in a book that only he, or someone who imitates his *Method*, can read.

---

[15] Étienne Gilson, *Reason and Revelation in the Middle Ages* (New York: Charles Scribner's Sons, 1938), 65. I thank James V. Schall, S. J. (r.i.p.) for recalling this passage to my attention; see his article, "Possessed of Both a Reason and a Revelation," in Peter A. Redpath (ed.), *A Thomistic Tapestry: Essays in Memory of Étienne Gilson* (Amsterdam and Atlanta: Editions Rodopi, B. V., 2002).

Chapter 1: Editor's Introduction

During the twelfth century, Averroes had constructed a sophistic argument to safeguard the rights and freedom of philosophy against intrusion by theologians and others and to protect Islam against heresies that a weak understanding of philosophy is prone to generate. This sophistic argument consisted of distinguishing three categories of human minds and three corresponding degrees and limits of human understanding, learning, and teaching "of one single and same truth": (1) the most true and abstract scientific mind of the philosopher, which supposedly apprehends, learns, and teaches this truth in an absolute sense in its hidden, interior meaning, through demonstrative reasoning "from the necessary to the necessary by the necessary"; (2) the less true and symbolic unscientific mind of the logician, and theologian, which grasps this truth in its exterior, imaginative, symbolic meaning, through logical interpretation and probability; and (3) the simple religious and believing mind, which apprehends this one and same truth through the imagination, emotions, and oratorical arguments.

Gilson explained that, while Averroes claimed, "the Koran is truth itself," he maintained that the Koran "has an exterior and symbolic meaning for the uninstructed, an interior and hidden meaning for scholars." He considered revelation's true meaning to be its most lofty meaning. Its most lofty meaning was its philosophical, or scientific, meaning.

Averroes thought that philosophical truth is "the highest type of human truth." This means that, for Averroes: (1) human truth is the highest type of Koranic truth; (2) the highest type of human truth is philosophy, or science; (3) philosophical, or scientific, truth is present in a hidden fashion in the Koran, and (4) only philosophers can recognize it![16]

Unhappily for subsequent philosophical history, I maintain that: (1) Petrarch took and adapted Averroes's division of human minds by designing his own program and method for *harmonizing religion and philosophy* and a new, fabricated interpretation of philosophy and its history to support it: (2) *mutatis mutandis*, Descartes unwittingly adopted Petrarch's program and method, and a new interpretation of philosophy and its history to support it; and (3) *mutatis mutandis*, to correct weaknesses in Descartes's system, by introducing his own trinitarian hierarchy of three categories of human minds and limits of human understanding, Rousseau accepted and modified the program and method of Descartes and Petrarch, and introduced a new interpretation of philosophy and its history to support it.

In Petrarch's program a new mind and profession replaced the trinitarian hierarchy of Averroes. In Petrarch's scheme, the highest form of human mind is that of theologizing poets (*poetae theologisantes*), not the mind of philosophers. As a complement of this new mind in the order of teaching and learning, Petrarch created a new profession of poetry that combines the techniques of rhetoric, poetry, and theology: *theologia poetica* (poetic theology).

In short, Petrarch appears simply to have attempted to use dialectical arguments and reductionism to defeat the claims of Averroes. He accepted the truth of Averroes's premise that the whole of

---

[16] Gilson, *History of Christian Philosophy in the Middle Ages*, 218–219.

Chapter 1: Editor's Introduction

truth is a hidden teaching, or body of knowledge; but he sought to drive Averroes's teaching into an opposite and an unwelcome conclusion by claiming that this truth is contained in the Book of Nature, which only the theologizing poet, not the philosopher, had the capacity to read.

From the standpoint of the prevailing, contemporary Western view of the relationship between philosophy and science, crucial to understand is that, in attempting to reform Descartes's view of systematic science, by using an analogous sort of dialectical argument against Descartes to that used by Petrarch against Averroes, Rousseau shakes hands across the centuries with Petrarch and Averroes. Descartes had reformed Petrarch's teaching by claiming that the whole of science exists completely within the human mind as a system of clear and distinct ideas; but only a person of exceptional ability, like Descartes, could recognize it. Recognizing that Descartes could not explain how mind and matter interact, Rousseau attempted to solve this problem by getting rid of Descartes's notion of matter and of Descartes's claims that, through application of simple Cartesian doubt, we find the system of science whole and complete in our minds and that only the Cartesian can read it.

To effect his goal, Rousseau: (1) reduced matter to spirit and (2) conceived Descartes's scientific system of clear and distinct ideas as initially obscure but spiritually-and-historically-emerging, in a neo-Averroistic mental trinity, through the ideas of tolerance, progress, and the voice of conscience. For Rousseau scientific truth historically evolves, is the evolution of historical consciousness, and only the Enlightened, tolerant mind can read this history.

While Rousseau accepted Descartes's claim that science is a system of clear and distinct ideas, Rousseau rejected Descartes's contention that God had buried this system in our minds simultaneously whole in the present, and that truth consists in simple will-power. Instead, Rousseau maintained that God has intended this system of science to emerge from the human race, under the influence of the voice of conscience, or tolerance, through progressive self-development, or "progress." In short, truth consists in the socialist will-to-power.

Rousseau contended that conscience is a way of speaking: an oracle, or voice, that moves us to project our emotions in increasingly unselfish, 'tolerant' ways across three stages of development: from being a child of mechanical instinct, to being a moral agent, to becoming a fully social civic being. For Rousseau, knowledge, science, true communication between substances, are simply the long-term result of projected emotion, of an increasingly socialistic will to, and extension of, emotional power. As he saw it, the voice of conscience is God's voice, free speech, an act of increasing states of tolerance or compassion whereby human nature emotionally emerges, or evolves, beyond a more primitive mechanical system of selfish individualism to an imperfectly social and moral stage, to, finally, a perfectly political social system of true science.

Rousseau realized that conscience in the proper sense (scientific will) cannot exist prior to the existence of knowledge and reason, the civic stage of complete Enlightenment. Where no truth exists, strictly speaking, no real conscience, freedom, or human communication exists. Like Descartes, Rousseau conflated truth and science and, like Descartes and Nietzsche, he located truth in an act of strong will, or emotion. For him, prior to the existence of real human science, no human truth exists. Hence, before humanity reaches its final stage of total social inclusion, a kind of totalitarian or collectivist civil will, scientific Enlightenment, Rousseau held that what we call 'conscience' is a primitive, mechanical-like groping toward the human good; and no real, *scientific* will or true freedom exists.

Only the Enlightened system of ideas (global socialism effected by the General Will) can make conscience (emotive, individual will) fully emerge. Because non-Enlightened ideas (1) are obscure and indistinct feelings and (2) cannot produce audible sound, they can produce no real communication, no real free speech. Rousseau maintained that such ideas generate the counterfeit noise of fanatics. Hence, prior to the new Enlightenment political world order, conscience and true freedom had no voice. No real free speech or human communication, existed. Strictly speaking, human beings were not scientific, not free; and no true, or social, justice could exist.

Rousseau maintained that the voice of conscience maturely develops as a result of a system of human emotions (sensations of the self as a body) feeling themselves together, emerging, into a system of other, self-disclosed, individual emotions (the idea of self as spirit). Union of these two systems of emotion generates the voice we call 'conscience': a voice that moves us to transport ourselves from one system into another, from a child of mechanical instinct to a moral agent, to a civic being.

For Rousseau, the voice of conscience, God's voice, is the act of free speech, an act of disclosure whereby the system of nature transports itself (human nature), according to a neo-Averroistic mental trinity, beyond a more primitive mechanical system to a social and, finally, political system. Conscience does this by changing the way we talk (just as a male's voice changes as he enters adolescence) as we move from the lower stage to the higher.

At the mechanical stage of human instinct, which corresponds to Averroes's totally imaginative and emotional level of the ordinary believer, persuaded only by oratorical arguments, Rousseau thinks that God's voice (conscience) speaks through the mechanical voice of human instinct, human nature viewed as a dumb animal, or machine.

At the moral stage of educational development, which corresponds to Averroes's second stage of symbolic mind of the logician and theologian, God's voice still speaks through the Book of Nature. But the Book of Nature is humanity emerged toward the first, primitive stage of Enlightenment reason and Scientific will, not the book of mechanical human instinct. At this point, the system of Enlightened ideas enables God, for the first time in human history, to utter his voice, and make it heard by the human spirit, not just by the body. That is, human beings get a taste of spirit, of freedom!

Rousseau uses the idea of tolerance to conflate the disciplines of metaphysics and politics and reduce the moral and political principle of justice to an epistemological tool serving a political project: to effect a state of higher metaphysical and historical consciousness, a state of Enlightened socialist feeling and Enlightened reading of history which, in our time, in some quarters, appears to be increasingly becoming the chief end of science. *In short, in Rousseau's hands, the classical theoretical discipline of metaphysics becomes reduced to a hermeneutic for reading history serving as a handmaid for effecting a practical political agenda: global socialism.*[17]

Chiefly because of the work of Rousseau, Descartes's dream of the monopoly of the mathematician alone over the whole of science of the universe did not last long. Chiefly through the writings of Rousseau, Enlightenment thinkers started to realize that Descartes's project to ground science as a logical system of clear and distinct ideas buried in the mind was a failure.

Hence, following Rousseau, and under the influence Newton, Enlightenment intellectuals like Immanuel Kant (b. 1724; d. 1804) and Georg Hegel (b. 1770; d. 1831) started to view the attempt to establish science as a social system of clear and distinct ideas to be the human project, a chief end of human life, an essential part of the human spirit's call of conscience and practical reason to cause the human spirit to emerge from conditions of religious backwardness.

The modern and Enlightenment reduction of science and truth to the social system of mathematical physics politically justified by the hermeneutic of tolerance in service to the socialist state is without intellectual justification. Apart from universal feeling that some higher, more-inclusive social feeling, a kind of neo-Averroistic, socialist intellect shared by 'tolerant' people collectively establishes truth, it has no criterion of truth. It is little more than Enlightenment intellectual relativism, neo-sophistry: a myth.

Rousseau looks to me as if he knew this. In his hands 'tolerant' people occupy the analogous position of Averroes's philosopher

---

[17] Redpath, Redpath, *Masquerade of the Dream Walkers: Prophetic Theology from the Cartesians to Hegel*, 67–99.

(and the separated possible intellect that knows through him), Petrarch's theologizing poets, Descartes's extraordinary man of pure reason, Newton's magi and prophets, Kant's Enlightened intellectual, Hegel's World Historical person, Marx's proletariat, and the liberal arts as handmaidens to higher learning. In his hands, science, philosophy, and wisdom become reduced to being in the right historical state of mind, having the right feelings about accepting any and all differences that the new possible intellect of Enlightened intellectuals at any time collectively dictate.

In his famous *Social Contract*, Rousseau simply analogously transposes Averroes's teaching about the unity of the scientific soul (a single, separated intellect that knows whatever truth humans know) from the order of theoretical to practical reason, thereby transforming Averroes's single human intellect for the entire human race into the General Will of the political body: a social will. *By so doing Rousseau gave birth to modern utopian and scientific socialism and its tendency to deny the reality of individual freedom and individual intelligence just as Averroes had denied the existence of knowledge, science, and freedom to the individual mind and the existence of the individual soul after death.*[18]

---

[18] Redpath, *Masquerade of the Dream Walkers: Prophetic Theology Theology from the Cartesians to Hegel*, 101–248. For a more detailed analysis of the how, wittingly or unwittingly, the thinking of Averroes and Petrarch influenced Rousseau, see Peter A. Redpath, "Petrarch's Dream and the Failed Modern Project: A Chapter Gilson Did not Write," part 1 of 2, in *Contemporary Philosophy*, 25, nn. 5–6 (2003), 3–9; part 2 of 2, in *Contemporary Philosophy*, 25, nn. 5-6 (2003), 52–57. I thank Karl-Heinz Nusser from the Universität München for suggesting that I add to my analysis of the influence of Averroes on Rousseau some mention of how my

Rousseau's influence on Kant is legendary. Kant considered Rousseau to be another Newton. He claimed that just as Newton had completed the science of external nature and laid bare the order and regularity of the external world, Rousseau had discovered the hidden nature of man.

Rousseau's teachings about tolerance heavily influenced Kant's political writings, especially his famous work, *An Answer to the Question 'What is Enlightenment?'* Kant's political writings, views about Enlightenment, in turn, heavily influenced Hegel, who heavily influenced Karl Marx (b. 1818; d. 1883).[19] In this way, I maintain Rousseau's teaching about human knowledge and science gradually became the chief influence for the emergence of a neo-Averroistic understanding of science and an essential union between science and utopian socialism in the West in our time.

Ultimately, today, the reduction of 'science' to positivistic science is essentially wedded to, depends upon, utopian socialism as its imitation of a metaphysical foundation. Today, a neo-Averroism inherited from Rousseau and the disordered understanding of tolerance that this neo-Averroism essentially employs as its hermeneutic for reading history has gradually become in the West the only means for scientifically and philosophically understanding politics, ethics, and truth in general.

---

thesis applies in the case of Rousseau's political teaching in his *Social Contract*.

[19] For a more detailed consideration of Rousseau's influence on Kant and Hegel, see Redpath, *Masquerade of the Dream Walkers: Prophetic Theology from the Cartesians to Hegel*, 67–229.

Henceforth, serious concern about traditional metaphysical and moral issues about who we are as human beings, how we originated, what life is all about, and what is our ultimate destiny are supposed to be left to Enlightened, utopian-socialist intellectuals, intellectuals schooled in the methods of modern mathematical physics. They are not to be left to speculation of untrained specialists, to petty, bourgeois, philistine, individualists as a Marxist might say.[20]

4. Why recovering a proper understanding of metaphysics is essential to restoring a proper understanding of philosophy, science, and their essential relation to wisdom

In my opinion, the disembodied reason of Descartes, the depersonalized, collectivist reason promoted by Rousseau, and the anti-contemplative reductionism of modern and contemporary physical 'science' falsely-so-called are foundational elements of the murderous depersonalization promoted by modern utopian, and scientific, socialism like Nazism, Fascism, and Marxism. Having a view of human reason totally out of contact with reality, these thinkers and the Enlightenment socialists they spawned, had no way of properly understanding real, individual, human relationships: individual, free, rational, living, loving acts. They had no way of comprehending hu-

---

[20] For how Rousseau's understanding of tolerance is currently being used by contemporary socialists to influence the direction of the contemporary world, see Peter A. Redpath, "Reduction of Justice to Tolerance in the New Totalitarian World Order," in *Telos*, n. 157 (2011), 185–192.

man beings as metaphysical, contemplative beings, or moral or political agents. According to all these thinkers, outside of mathematically-measurable data, or mechanistically- or socialistically-controlled events, no truth exists about the physical universe that real human beings inhabit and no real relations that exist in that world are comprehensible.

For the purpose of understanding the main arguments of this essay, a need exists to comprehend that the metaphysical principles that underlie the prevailing, contemporary, Western understanding of science and its development are not philosophical. They are sophistic principles of human nature, conscience, and natural law; chiefly ideological, propagandistic, principles derived from Rousseau's sophistic, utopian dream of human nature, science, and happiness. Strictly speaking, no rational justification exists to reduce the whole of philosophy, science, wisdom, and truth to the procedures of the contemporary social system of mathematical physics. Such a reduction is founded upon a rationally unjustified assumption, nothing else.

Hence, if we want to transcend this fideistic, Enlightenment mindset, and the murderous, utopian socialism that exists chiefly to justify it, in place of the disordered understandings of human reason that Enlightenment intellectuals mistakenly claimed to be the metaphysical foundations of philosophy, science, wisdom, and truth, then the acting person (the sentient, embodied individual actively engaged in free, personal, living relationships) must once again become a founding, metaphysical principle of philosophy, science. In place of some collectivist mass, disembodied spirit, or collection of mechanistically-controlled individuals as the foundation of scientific understanding, to re-establish the proper union between wisdom and science, the West needs to re-establish primacy of the individual, sentient being engaged in personal action as a first principle of knowing, truth, science, philosophy, and wisdom.

Moreover, a need exists to recognize that our contemporary Western educational institutions and the socialist political regimes that give birth to and support these gulags are necessary effects of the application to the practical order of Enlightenment sophistry about the nature of philosophy, science, wisdom, and truth: of the political attempt to reduce the whole of knowledge to a social-system-science of historically-emerging clear and distinct ideas.

In short, mainly under the influence of Descartes's and Rousseau's disordered metaphysical understandings of science, philosophy, wisdom, and truth, the Enlightenment project unwittingly gave birth to educational institutions that are institutes of sophistry, essentially socialistic forms of propaganda and secularized fideism. These arose as the necessary means for engendering a poetic, metaphysical myth in the form of utopian history that the whole of science, philosophy, wisdom, and truth are contained in the story, 'narrative,' about the birth and development of the practical science of modern physics, which only the socialistically-minded, mathematical physicist, like a shaman or oracle can supposedly comprehend.

Under the influence of Descartes, Rousseau, and their progeny, modern physics sought to be intellectually all-consuming, to be the only form of human learning, of human truth. No rational argument can justify this quixotic quest. So, the modern 'scientific' spirit turned to poetic myth, sophistry, *fairy-tale history*, and fideistic spirituality to create the metaphysical arguments it needed rationally to justify its all-consuming nature. In practical terms, this means that, if universities are primarily institutes of higher education, and metaphysics is the highest form of natural human education, the modern scientific spirit necessarily inclined Western intellectuals to create propaganda institutes, and political regimes that support the existence of such institutes, to justify modern mathematical physics's false claim that it is the only form of human knowledge, science, and wisdom about the universe.

Most critics of modernity today correctly call these neo-gnostic, fideistic, principles 'secular humanism.' Precisely speaking, they wrongly call them 'philosophy,' 'science.' Educationally, under the influence of Rousseau, these sophistic principles maintain that all learning is revelation, or disclosure, of the something that re- places the traditional Western creator-God, of something they call the 'human spirit.' By 'human spirit' they mean a universal scientific spirit (the spirit of progress, true human freedom, the human project: the utopian-socialist will-to-power) that grows by first revealing itself in forms of backward Scriptural writings and organized religious practices: the same sort of universal, anti-Catholic, anti-Semitic spirit that was a main cause of the development of Fascism, Nazism, and Marxism.

For their adherents, metaphysics is the epic poetic story, an Enlightened, *fairy-tale history*, about the evolution, or emergence, of human consciousness, the universal human spirit ('true science') from backward states of selfishness and primitive religions like Judaism and Catholicism, to that of a new political world order dominated by Enlightened systematic science and the religion of love of humanity, 'secular humanism.' And tolerance is this mythical history's chief engine of progress, story-telling, and means of reading history.

The means of such emergence consists of a synthesis of what Rousseau calls the 'voice of conscience' (which he conflates with natural law) and poetic enthusiasm, or, more simply, 'tolerance,' an increasingly inclusive socialist feeling for love of humanity, an increasing willingness to incorporate all human differences into a higher state of socialist, political consciousness as a means for achieving the political goal of world socialism: for everyone to think in the same neo-Averroistic way Enlightened intellectuals think.

Traditional Western universities, classical liberal arts, the classical understanding of philosophy, natural law, individual liberty, the dignity of the individual human being, and republican government, individual rights, and families are unsuitable handmaidens for generating, growing, and sustaining these myths. Needed are imperious, centralized bureaucracies.

To defeat these myths, Westerners need: (1) a radically different approach to philosophy and science: one that insists on the existence of forms in physical things, including that of a soul within the human person; and (2) a return to an educational philosophy rooted in human beings possessing human faculties that become maturely developed through human habituation.

A necessary condition for the start of such a recovery program is that, like the utopian addicts we are, Westerners must bottom out and recognize that: (1) what my friend and colleague John N. Deely (r.i.p.) rightly called 'postmodernism falsely-so-called' is simply modernism on steroids and essentially out of touch with reality; and (2) we cannot build, or recover, a culture based upon the conviction that no real communication exists between substances. As Deely well said in his monograph, *Semiotic Animal: A Postmodern Definition of 'Human Being' Transcending Patriarchy and Feminism*, "Just as in politics you cannot effect a revolution and at the same time preserve the *ancien régime*, so in intellectual culture you cannot develop what is new simply by repeating what is old."[21]

If we want to transcend depersonalization in contemporary science, we have to transcend the Babelism of modern thought that is essentially related to the denial of the existence of individually existing human beings naturally capable of communicating with each other independently of social science and the utopian, socialist state. We have to restore wisdom to science because, absent wisdom, strictly speaking, science cannot be science. In such a situation, scientific reason becomes displaced by sophistry, intellectual malpractice, propaganda, myth: utopian dreams.

Once we understand that we properly (most precisely) name things through their proximate causes, and that, in the case of arts and sciences, in a complete sense, we properly attribute art or science to someone because that person's actions are being performed

---

[21] John N. Deely, *Semiotic Animal: A Postmodern Definition of 'Human Being' Transcending Patriarchy and Feminism* (South Bend, Indiana: St. Augustine's Press, 2010), 10.

through a habit or virtue that perfects a person and a person's operations, what passes as science from an observer's point of view can become a form of malpractice from a practitioner's point of view.

If a person with the knowledge of medicine misuses that knowledge intentionally to make patients sick, strictly speaking, that person is no scientist, no physician. The proximate principle of that person's actions is malevolence, intellectual bastardization, not art or science; moral vice, not intellectual virtue. If this is true of a physician falsely-so-called, it is equally true of a mathematician falsely-so-called and physicist falsely-so-called. Hence, strictly speaking, many contemporary mathematicians and physicists, even leading ones, are not scientists. They are shamans.

To claim that the whole of truth is contained in the science of medicine is absurd. Equally absurd is to claim that the whole of truth is contained in mathematics, or mathematical physics.

The mere fact that a person has a facility to make right judgments about a subject does not, in and of itself, strictly speaking, qualify a person to merit the title 'scientist,' which, strictly speaking, is only merited by the possession of the habit of science. Knowledge that has become divorced from wisdom tends to degenerate into a tool of malevolence, tends to divorce itself from right relation to other forms of human knowledge and become despotic. To claim that mathematics or mathematical physics is the measure of all truth is simply a modern version of the intellectual imperialism of Protagoras (b. 490 BC; d. 420 BC). Its intellectual foundation is non-existent. The claim is a piece of pure sophistry.

No medical knowledge that conceived of itself as being the whole of human truth could rightly claim to understand the nature of medicine. Many human beings would rightly judge such a grandiose claim to border on delusion, madness. Should not the same be true of a mathematics or mathematical physics that made such a disingenuous, imperious claim?

As Aristotle and St. Thomas understood centuries ago, by nature, human reason tends to rule politically (that is, justly), not despotically, over those human faculties that are naturally inclined to follow its directions. But this is true only of human reason rightly conceived. When a qualitatively subordinate science, like mathematics, or physics, attempts to displace a qualitatively higher science and, beyond this, to reduce the whole of truth and wisdom to its subject-matter and methods, such a project cannot be effected through rational persuasion. Ultimately, it must seek to effect such rule through coercion, propaganda, despotism, the blind will (better, urge) to power.

The human intellectual faculties are naturally inclined to cooperate with each other, and other human faculties, to help human beings become happy. This is one reason that, by nature, the human soul generates an order of arts and sciences. To be complete as science knowledge must do more than facilitate right judgment about its specific subject matter. It must also, simultaneously, contribute to the perfection of a human being as a whole. If one human science/philosophy becomes incapable of co-existing with other forms of human science/philosophy, even seeks to destroy them, something is rotten in the kingdom of science, philosophy, and needs to be corrected. Such a 'science,' 'philosophy,' is no science, philosophy, at all.

If, correctly understood, science, philosophy, is chiefly a habit, virtue, of the human intellect (which is a faculty of the human soul), any science, philosophy, that denies the existence of the human soul and intellectual habits and virtues cannot correctly understand its own nature and be what it claims to be. Moreover, if intellectual habits and virtues are psychological qualities that relate different intellectual faculties to each other and to the world around us, destruction of the notion of science, philosophy, as a human habit, virtue, of the human soul must completely disorder the real relation of human faculties to each other and of human beings to the physical world around us. The cumulative effect of this disorder will ultimately be total inability of a human being rightly to relate to anything.

5. How my present critique of contemporary 'science,' 'philosophy' largely repeats and synthesizes criticisms made by several twentieth- and twenty-first-century intellectuals

Unhappily, the complaint I have lodged against the imperious nature of contemporary 'science,' 'philosophy,' is, in large part, nothing new. Most of what I have said above I have gathered from twentieth-century intellectuals like Mortimer J. Adler (b. 1902; d. 2001), Jacques Maritain (b. 1882; d. 1973), Étienne Gilson, and Pope Benedict XVI. In fact, knowingly or not (I suspect knowingly), the Vatican's recent admonition about the dangers of scientific positivism largely repeat critiques made by these intellectuals during the 1930s and 1940s.

Chief examples of such critiques are Adler's articles "This Prewar Generation," and "God and the Professors" in which Adler criticized American university professors, educators, and Deweyan "pragmatic-liberals" for producing a generation of American youth incapable of intellectually defending the principles of American democracy against Adolf Hitler's (b. 1889; d. 1945) program of Nazi socialism.[22]

In "This Prewar Generation," published in *Harper's Magazine* in October 1940, Adler described American youth of the 1930s and early 1940s as: (1) appearing to have "grown up with no allegiances, no "moral philosophy to renounce"; (2) people who talk like "calloused realists"; (3) "having a distrust of any cause which spoke the language of principles"; (4) lacking a faith in democracy equal to that of Hitler's Nazi youth's faith in Fascism.[23]

---

[22] Mortimer J. Adler, "This Prewar Generation," in Geraldine van Doren (ed.), *Mortimer J. Adler, Reforming Education: The Opening of the American Mind* (New York: Macmillan Publishing Company and London, England: Collier Macmillan Publishers, 1988), 4–5; "God and the Professors," Part One, in Max Weismann (ed.), *The Great Ideas Online*, 629 (August 11, 2011), 6–12 and "God and the Professors," Part Two, in *The Great Ideas Online*, 629 (August 11, 2011), 1–12. I thank my friend Max Weismann (r.i.p.) former director and co-founder with Mortimer J. Adler of the Center for the Study of Great Ideas, for providing me with a copy of this article.

[23] Adler, "This Prewar Generation," 4–5.

Adler observed how, concerned about preparedness for war, commencement speakers in June 1940 "all spoke with amazing uniformity" about the dangers of the moral and political disaffection of American youth. "In their impatience, however sincere," Adler noted, these speakers "committed a basic error in rhetoric. They did not even ask themselves why all their words would fall upon deaf ears, why stirring words would not stir, why even the loftiest visions would not inspire."[24]

Adler claimed the reason such words fell upon deaf ears was that the speakers had forgotten that we can only control effects by altering causes. Based upon his then fifteen years of teaching experience, he proposed the thesis that the reason why American college students and recent graduates did not take any moral, economic, or political problem seriously was chiefly because "they are sophists in the most invidious sense of the term, which connotes an unqualified skepticism about all moral judgments."[25] Adler maintained that "their only principle is that there are no moral principles at all, their only slogan that all statements of policy, all appeals to standards, are nothing but slogans, and hence frauds and deceptions."[26]

In the political arena, Adler said that such skepticism reduces to the mindset of the ancient sophist Thrasymachos that justice is the advantage of the stronger, might makes right; with the exception that American students could not make, or defend, the case as intelligently and as could old Thrasymachos.

---

[24] Adler, "This Prewar Generation," 5.
[25] Adler, "This Prewar Generation," 7.
[26] Adler, "This Prewar Generation," 7.

Adler laid the blame for immunization of American youth against the ability to defend democracy as a form of government intrinsically superior to Fascism clearly on the "scientific" mindset that dominated American higher education, on the shoulders of American college and university professors who had reduced the whole of truth to positivistic science.

He maintained, further, that this mindset had not arisen overnight, was not the peculiar creation of the preceding generation. He claimed, "What has been happening in American education since 1900, what has finally achieved its full effect in the present generation, flows with tragic inevitability from the seeds of modem culture as they have developed in the past three hundred years. The very things which constituted the cultural departure that we call modern times have eventuated, not only in the perverted education of American youth today, but also in the crises they are unprepared to face."[27]

What Adler saw arising in American education since 1900 was a form of utopian socialism that Lewis Mumford (b. 1895; d. 1990) had labeled "pragmatic liberalism."[28] Adler considered as a "historical accident" the ascendancy of this mindset in the U. S. simultaneously with the rise of Fascism in Europe. But, he added, "Only the timing is a coincidence" because "the European and the American maladies arise from the same causes" are "the last fruitions of modern man's exclusive trust in science and his gradual disavowal of

---

[27] Adler, "This Prewar Generation," 7.
[28] Adler, "This Prewar Generation," 7–9.

whatever lies beyond the field of science as irrational prejudice, as opinion emotionally held."[29]

In making this claim, Adler was careful not to make 'science' his essay's 'villain.' The villain, he claimed, was the intellectual and practical misuse of science. He said:

> We do not blame science for the murderous tools it has enabled men to make; neither should we blame science, or for that matter scientists, for the destructive doctrines men have made in its name, men who are for the most part philosophers and educators, not scientists. All these doctrines have a common center—positively, the exclusive adoration of science; negatively, the denial that philosophy or theology can have any independent authority. We can regard this intellectual misuse of science as another one of the false modern religions—the religion of science, closely related to the religion of the state. We can group all these doctrines together and call them by names which have become current: positivism and scientism. And again we can see a deep irony in the historic coincidence that just when the practical misuse of science has armed men for wholesale slaughter, scientism—the intellectual misuse of science—has all but disarmed them morally.[30]

---

[29] Adler, "This Prewar Generation," 9.
[30] Adler, "This Prewar Generation," 9.

Chapter 1: Editor's Introduction

While Adler was right not to blame 'science' for being the villain of his essay, I maintain he was wrong to call "misuse of science" the culprit because, as he recognized when describing American college students as invidious "sophists," the proper proximate cause of their behavior was sophistry, not science. Science could not have been misused by them because science did not exist in them. If science is a psychological virtue, a virtue of the human soul present in the human intellect, divorcing science from any moral standards and philosophical metaphysics, wisdom (as these students had done), essentially disorders the human intellect and makes the practice of science impossible.

Science, philosophy, started to rise with the ancient Greeks when the ancient physicists, like philosophy's Father, Thales (fl. 585 BC) began to recognize: (1) the existence of secondary causes, natures, in physical things; (2) that knowledge and wisdom were not the sole property of the gods, but were natural achievements of the human mind; (3) mystery exists that can cause sense wonder; and (4) that this natural wonder can be put to rest through thoroughly-natural, virtuous, reflection of the human intellect made in conjunction with the human sense faculties of the human soul.

Modern 'science,' 'philosophy,' is rooted in the Rousseauan conviction that: (1) no natures, secondary causes (forms, including souls) exist in physical things; (2) no mysteries exist in physical reality; (3) strictly speaking, no physical reality exists: only *spirit* exists and is active; (4) the human spirit is God; (5) all human knowledge is an act of revelation; (6) science is a necessary condition of virtue and ethics; virtue and ethics are not necessary conditions of science; and (7) no human soul exists in which habits or virtues could exist.

In a way, in his "This Prewar Generation," Adler recognized that sophistry, not misuse of science, was the villain of his story when he said what he called the misuse of science was "another one of the false modern religions—the religion of science, closely related to the religion of the state."[31] Confounding science with religion, state religion, is not to misuse science; it is to misunderstand science, to mistake science for something it is not: an act of revelation; which is precisely what Rousseau and his progeny in 'social science' have done. In so doing, a person does not misuse science in the sense of putting science to wrong use. A person displaces science and virtue with propaganda.

Moreover, since modernity has essentially displaced science, transformed what had been science into a kind of state religion, Adler is somewhat wrong to see the simultaneous existence of Fascism and pragmatic liberalism as a historical accident. If I am right, and the contemporary understanding of science is rooted in Rousseauean, utopian socialism, the rise of contemporary 'science' in American education presupposed the existence of a socialistic mindset among American educators as a necessary condition for the existence of contemporary 'science.' While the fact that American socialism was pragmatic liberalism and not full-blown Fascism might have been a historical accident, that this mindset was socialistic was no accident. As Adler well knew, John Dewey (b. 1854; d. 1952) was the chief source of this way of thinking; and Dewey was largely recycling the socialism of Rousseau.

---

[31] Adler, "This Prewar Generation," 9.

In his article Adler made other mistakes. For example, he claimed: (1) "We do not blame science for the murderous tools it has enabled men to make"; and (2) "neither should we blame science, or for that matter scientists, for the destructive doctrines men have made in its name, men who are for the most part philosophers and educators, not scientists."[32]

Science did not enable men to make murderous tools. Lack of science, divorce of science from wisdom, morality, intellectual and moral virtue, did so. Science presupposes the existence of a moral culture rooted in minimum levels of professional honesty and justice as a necessary condition for its existence. A medical doctor who uses knowledge of medicine to murder is practicing murder, not the art of medicine; is using knowledge (not the science) of medicine to carry out his crime. Moreover, science can only be science if it derives its first principles from the being of intellectually independent beings and virtues of the intellectual soul, if science is an act of this individual knower using as first principles natural knowledge of the being of things, not myth, superstition, or propaganda (even Enlightenment propaganda).

Hence, Adler was right to complain about "the exclusive adoration of" what he misnamed 'science,' as "one of the false modern religions." He was wrong, however, to call this false modern religion the religion of 'science.'

The mere fact that a person possesses knowledge, arrives at right conclusions, does not mean a person has done so by means of art or science. The person could just as well have done so through fraud,

---

[32] Adler, "This Prewar Generation," 9.

deceit, experience, cleverness, guessing, or knowledge. A student who arrives at right answers by cheating is no artist or scientist. Neither is a prophet; and, despite what Descartes mistakenly claimed, not every act of knowing is an act of science.

The contemporary reduction of the whole of knowledge and science to mathematical physics (to what Adler and many others call 'positivism,' 'scientism') is a myth, chiefly the effect of a moral disorder, a political project: a moral refusal to admit that true science must have its initial foundation in intellectual virtue and evident, *per se nota*, principles that only a philosophical metaphysics (not utopian socialism or propaganda) can rationally justify. Divorcing itself from a rational foundation in intellectual virtue and philosophical metaphysics, and an essential connection to the generic end of all science to promote human happiness, destroys the claim of any intellectual activity to be scientific or philosophical.

As Aristotle maintained and Plato recognized, science is more than knowledge of the fact: knowledge of the reasoned fact.[33] Science involves the habitual ability to explain why something is what it is, what chiefly causes this or that. This is true even in the case of answers to 'how' questions, which, when considered precisely, necessarily involve 'what' questions (for example, when I ask how to do something, I am asking what to do). Absent such habitual ability to give a reasoned explanation of why something is what it is, what we misname 'science' is no more science than the epic poetry of the ancient Greeks.

---

[33] See Plato, *Meno*, 97A–98B; see Aristotle, *Posterior Analytics*, Bk 1, ch. 11, 77a5–9.

Chapter 1: Editor's Introduction

If the ultimate reason that mathematical physics is supposedly the whole of science and measure of all truth is that Zeus says it is so, mathematical physics has no rational foundation. Why, then, should it have a rational foundation when the ultimate reason given for its imperious nature is that the utopian, socialist state, the collectivist human spirit, the law courts, or that contemporary 'scientific experts' declare it is so?

No matter how precisely a person could predict the future using numbers, if that person were to say that the reason he was so good with his predictions was that numbers are revelations, bits of news from the spirit world, no rational human being would conclude that this person's exceptional intellectual ability was an act of science. If such be the case, why should any of us conclude that the mode or reasoning that Enlightenment intellectuals inherited from Rousseau and have tried to pass off to modernity as science" merits the name 'science'? According to Rousseau, all human knowledge is news from the spirit world, projections of irrational feelings, blind emotions, which have magically grown into science through conflict with other, supposedly backward, religious emotions.

As Adler noted, one net effect of such sophistry is that, like the youth of America's pre-World War II generation, human beings start to develop a "distrust of all language."[34] Hence, just as I noted above about the mindset of most contemporary Western college students and Westerners in general, in the first part of the twenty-first century, Adler said students were convinced that: (1) only the methods of experimentation or empirical research generate valid

---

[34] Adler, "This Prewar Generation," 10.

knowledge of the nature of the universe and human beings; (2) questions we cannot answer by the methods of the natural and social sciences we cannot answer in any trustworthy or convincing way (or answers to such questions are arbitrary, unfounded, opinions); (3) the great achievement of the modern age is more than the accumulation of scientific knowledge: recognition of the positivistic method of empirical research and experimentation as the only dependable way to solve problems (in consequence, modern times have seen human "emancipation from the superstitions of religion, the dogmatisms of theology, and the armchair speculations of philosophers"); (4) study of social phenomena became scientific when research divorced itself entirely from normative principles, "when economists and students of politics no longer asked about the justice of social arrangements, but only who gets what, when, and how."[35]

Following Socrates' critique of Thrasymachos' claim that justice is the advantage of the stronger, and following what Plato's brother Glaucon says to Socrates shortly after the start of Book Two of Plato's *Republic*, Adler reasoned that, confronted by repeated exposure to such invidious rhetoric, a bright college student will readily conclude that: (1) moral questions cannot be answered by the methods of natural or social science; (2) in the domains of individual behavior and politics, except as expressions of personal prejudice, we cannot make 'value judgments'; (3) economics and politics have no essential connection to ethics.[36]

---

[35] Adler, "This Prewar Generation," 10.
[36] Adler, "This Prewar Generation," 11.

Following Thrasymachos' modern reincarnation, such a bright young student will become a disciple of Machiavelli, "as much a realist in politics as Hitler and Mussolini." And, "if, in addition to being bright," Adler added, "he is proud of his modernity, he will regard anyone who talks about standards of goodness, principles of justice, moral virtues as an unregenerate old fogey; and he will express his aversion for such outmoded opinions by the *ad hominem* use of epithets like 'medieval,'' or 'scholastic,' or 'mystic.'"[37]

Under the sheer weight of such indoctrination, Adler observed that college students of the 1930s and early 1940s came to dislike words like 'truth,' 'goodness,' because they sounded like "absolute values" so widely decried in social science departments at colleges and universities at the time.[38] (Quite understandable since modernity had essentially divorced science from any and all virtue and any and all human good.) He then lamented the fact that opposition "to the teaching pronounced in unison by the social scientists" was not opposed by philosophy departments at these same institutions.

Adler wrongly attributed this lack of opposition to what he considered to be the fact that the doctrine of scientism was "certainly the dominant dogma of American philosophy" at the time. He saw this dominance as part of "the degenerative tendency of modem philosophy to move in this direction that had reached its culmination in American pragmatism and all its sequelae—the numerous varieties of positivism." He maintained that all the varieties of modern

---

[37] Adler, "This Prewar Generation,"10–11; see Plato, *Republic*, Bk. 2, 361E–367E.

[38] Adler, "This Prewar Generation," 11.

philosophy "agree on one point: that only science gives us valid knowledge of reality."[39]

As a result, Adler concluded, "philosophy, at its best, can be nothing more than a sort of commentary on the findings of science; and at its worst, when it refuses to acknowledge the exclusive right of scientific method to marshal evidence and draw conclusions therefrom, philosophy is either mere opinion or nonsensical verbiage."[40] Within such a context, Adler rightly saw that, especially as recounting "primitive times before the scientific era" (that is, the seventeenth century), philosophy's history is told as a history of guesses, some bright, some wild, but all equally unworthy of modern credence."[41]

In short, instead of opposing the social scientists, members of 'Philosophy Departments' falsely-so-called championed their moral relativism. In 'philosophy' courses, Adler claimed "the student really learns how to argue like a sophist against all 'values' as subjective and relative. Far from being the last bulwark against the scientism professed or insinuated by every other part of the curriculum, the philosophy courses reinforce the negativism of this doctrine by inspiring disrespect for any philosophy which claims to be independent knowledge."[42]

To complete their job, Adler maintained that philosophy departments used semanticism (what his friend Jacques Maritain would later call 'Babelism') to implement the ancient sophistries that they

---

[39] Adler, "This Prewar Generation," 11.
[40] Adler, "This Prewar Generation," 11.
[41] Adler, "This Prewar Generation," 11–12.
[42] Adler, "This Prewar Generation," 12.

had revived. In these departments, Adler claimed students learned "to suspect all words, especially abstract words." They were told that "statements which cannot be scientifically verified are meaningless," that abstract words like 'justice,' 'right,' 'liberty,' 'happiness,' that enter into moral judgments "have only rhetorical meaning. Denuded of deceptive verbiage, all such judgments can be reduced to statements of what I like or what displeases me. There is no 'should' or 'ought.'"[43]

While Adler clearly understood the sophistic nature of "Philosophy' and 'Social Science' departments during his time, I find unfortunate that he would call modern 'Philosophy Departments' 'philosophical' and modern 'Social Science Departments 'scientific.' Most twentieth-century U.S. college and university 'Philosophy Departments' were not examples of "the degenerative tendency of modern philosophy" any more than the 'Social Science Departments' of the twentieth century were examples of the degenerative effects of modern 'social science.' They were and are prime examples the modern lack of philosophy and social science, of the degenerative cultural effects of neo-sophistry fulfilling its nature in modern culture under the rubrics of 'philosophy' and 'science.' Modern 'philosophy' is no more philosophy than modern 'social science' is science. Both are forms of neo-Protagorean sophistry. And their net effect tends to be 'Babelism'—the inability of human beings to communicate with each other.

---

[43] Adler, "This Prewar Generation," 12.

6. Why the future of Western culture and civilization essentially depends upon ending the separation between philosophy and science

As Adler observed in his article "God and the Professors," like the health and disease of the body, cultural health consists in the harmonious functioning of its parts, and cultures die from lack of harmonious functioning of these same parts. He added that "science, philosophy, and religion are certainly major parts of European culture; their distinction from one another as quite separate parts is certainly the most characteristic cultural achievement of modern times. But if they have not been properly distinguished, they cannot be properly related; and unless they are properly related, properly ordered to one another, cultural disorder, such as that of modern times, inevitably results."[44]

In short, if we do not properly understand the natures of things, we cannot properly relate and unite them as parts of a coherent whole. This, however, is precisely the problem we have with solving the decline of Western culture and civilization in our time. We do not properly understand the nature of philosophy and science, the way metaphysics essentially relates to both, and how, through this relation, metaphysics uses arts, philosophy, science, to generate cultures and civilizations.

Many modern 'scientists,' 'philosophers,' in fact, tend to glory in maintaining that things have no natures. Failing to understand the

---

[44] Adler, "God and the Professors," 12.

natures of things, we cannot properly understand the nature of religion and unite philosophy and science to religion to produce a healthy culture and civilization. Moreover, if the activity through which we unite parts is a state-sanctioned activity that essentially involves state-sanctioned sophists defining the state-sanctioned natures of things, the unity we generate we achieve by propaganda, myth, not science.

The chief reason we do not understand the nature of science and philosophy today results, as Adler says, from defects of our intellectual leaders, teachers, savants. "The disorder of modern culture is a disorder in their minds, a disorder which manifests itself in the universities they have built, in the educational system they have devised, in the teaching they do, and which, through that teaching, perpetuates itself and spreads out in ever widening circles from generation to generation."[45]

Such being the case, if we want to stop the decline of Western culture and civilization, we need to do a 'Hail Mary' pass over the contemporary intellectual hierarchy of the Enlightenment socialist state (of state-sanctioned sophists who dominate our colleges and universities) so that we can learn once again how to communicate with each other in properly scientific, philosophical, and religious ways.

As long ago as 1947, like Adler before him, in his Mexico City address to UNESCO, the great twentieth-century Catholic intellectual, Jacques Maritian, started to glimpse the need for the West to overcome the Babelism of modern culture, the inability of individual

---

[45] Adler, "God and the Professors," Part One, 9.

human beings naturally to be capable of communicating with each other independently of social science and the socialist state. At the time, he called for the Organization effectively to use education, science, and culture to contribute to international security and concrete work for peace among peoples.[46]

Maritain's address touched on solving five interrelated and historically-rooted problems that he considered necessary conditions to building a supranational community of peoples and the future work of peace: (1) absolute national sovereignty; (2) *Machiavellianism*; (3) *Realpolitik*; (4) transcending the Babelism of modern thought; and (5) reconciling wisdom and science, especially in modern technology.[47]

At the time, Maritain claimed that modern nation states absurdly presumed the right of absolute sovereignty trumps all other moral authority while, simultaneously, appealing to the contradictory doctrine of natural law to justify whatever they chose to do. He called the claim that politics should be indifferent to a real good and evil "a homicidal error" and such appeals to natural law intellectually incoherent.[48]

He added that only the right spiritual, the right moral and metaphysical, climate, one based upon a proper understanding of human

---

[46] Jacques Maritain, "Allocution du Président à la première séance plénière de la deuxième session de la Conférence générale de l'Unesco, 6 novembre 1947, Son Excellence Jacques Maritain, Chef de la Délégation française," in *Célébration du centenaire de la naissance de Jacques Maritain, 1882–1973*, no editor listed (New York: UNESCO, 1982), 9–33.

[47] Maritain, "Allocution du Président," 16–18.

[48] Maritain, "Allocution du Président," 11.

nature and capable of affirming the existence of real heroes, can produce that power of authentic political justice that can conquer the principle and power of Machiavellianism. He maintained that we will never achieve a stable and enduring peace in this world so long as, in the structures of civilization and human awareness, we maintain Babelism in human thought (the divorce between wisdom and science that Modern 'Philosophy's Father,' Descartes, had initiated) and we fail to start rigorously submitting the applications of science to moral right and the true ends of human life.[49]

Maritain thought that, to transcend the depersonalization in contemporary science, UNESCO needed to help the world recover a correct understanding of the human person and cultural truths from our classical ethical, metaphysical, and religious wisdom that support it.[50]

He reasoned that, given the contemporary world's widely differing theological and metaphysical traditions, on a practical level, appeal to the existence of a natural law would be the best way for peoples of the world today to come to some sort of common agreement about what we are as people, what is wisdom, and how we should go about reintegrating these notions into physical science. If a natural law truly exists, he reasoned, it will depend upon a common understanding of the human person, and we should reasonably expect to find evidence of its existence and the notion of the dignity of the person that supports it historically in the world body of common law.[51]

---

[49] Maritain, "Allocution du Président," 11.
[50] Maritain, "Allocution du Président," 13.
[51] Maritain, "Allocution du Président," 14–17.

While Maritain was engaging in such musings his French friend and philosophical colleague Étienne Gilson was musing about how some Westerners tend to be slow learners, have needed some time to grasp the full implications of the late modern project. At the close of World War II, Gilson claimed we in the West made our most astounding, involuntary, discovery: late modern science is essentially Nietszshean. "The great secret that science has just wrested from matter," Gilson observed, "is the secret of its destruction. To know today is synonymous with to destroy."

Gilson considered Nietzsche's declaration of God's death to be "the capital discovery of modern times," bigger than the explosion at Hiroshima. While Maritain was musing about how to use recognition of natural law to form common practical agreements among the world's people, Gilson thought that Nietzsche's declaration of God's death signaled a metaphysical revolution of the highest, widest, and deepest order in the West. Nietzsche is metaphysical dynamite. He knew it, readily admitted it.[52]

While Enlightened Westerners had gotten out of the habit of talking about things like 'divine law,' some, like Maritain, apparently still held onto its vestige in Enlightened, secularized appeals to "the voice of conscience" to solve the world's problems. But what will happen to us, Gilson asked, when more of us start to realize that the

---

[52] Étienne Gilson, *The Terrors of the Year 2000* (Toronto: St. Michael's College, 1949), 5, 14–16.; see Friedrich Nietzsche, "*Ecce Homo*," in Friedrich Nietzsche, *The Philosophy of Nietzsche*, no editor or translator listed (New York: Random House, Modern Library, 1954), 923–933. I thank my deceased colleague Richard Ingardia (r.i.p.) for first making me aware of this magnificent opuscule by Gilson.

modern voice of conscience (and, presumably, its principle: natural law) is the reflection of nothing, a convenient illusion we have created to maintain the intoxicating joy of our own poetic and sophistic project?[53]

Finding ourselves totally free to engage in the perpetual, Sisyphean task of endless self-creation, Gilson said, we resemble a soldier on a twenty-four hour leave with nothing to do: totally bored in the tragic loneliness of an idle freedom we cannot productively use. To Gilson's ears, the explosion of Hiroshima resounded a solemn metaphysical assertion of post-Nietzshean, late modern, man's statement that, while we no longer want to be God's image, we can still be God's caricature. While we cannot create anything, we now possess the intoxicating power to destroy everything.

As a result, feeling totally empty and alone, late modern man offers, to anyone willing to take it, the futile freedom he does not know how to use. "He is ready for all the dictators, leaders of these human herds who follow them as guides and who are all finally conducted by them to the same place—the *abbatoir*" (the slaughterhouse).[54] Having freed ourselves from divine rule, the necessary political consequence for 'postmodern man' falsely so-called is political enslavement by a totalitarian State. Having refused to serve God, we have no one left to judge the state, no arbiter between us and the state.[55]

---

[53] Gilson, *The Terrors of the Year 2000*, 28.

[54] Gilson, *The Terrors of the Year 2000*, 24.

[55] I thank John N. Deely for reminding me that postmodernism as popularly understood today is essentially (1) modernism in its natural stage of maturity: decay; and (2) should properly be called 'postmodernism falsely-so-called.'

As Gilson saw it, just after World War II, appeals to conscience helped some of us in the West, apparently Maritain included, to pretend not to understand the catastrophic consequences for the West and the world of the grandiose sophistry of the falsely-so-called 'postmodern' project: Our destiny has become "the absurd" and "truly exhausting task" of perpetual self-invention without model, purpose, or rule. Having turned ourselves into gods, Gilson maintained, we do not know what to do with our divinity.

Clearly, for Gilson, just as for Maritain, the terrors of the late modern world are, in root cause, 'modern, moral, and metaphysical; but, for Gilson, the chief clash of civilizations we face today is not between the politics of West and East, or the West and other political orders, between the Western tradition and other metaphysical and religious traditions. It is a metaphysical and moral clash between the ancient and modern West.

No wonder exists why this current conflict has become an essential effect of modern 'science' falsely-so-called. Having essentially divorced itself from all moral and intellectual virtue, including wisdom and happiness, having reduced all these to its all-consuming method, like modern economics and politics, modern 'science' has essentially divorced itself from all real human good and the chief end of human life: the creator-God. As a contrary of real science, modern 'science' has embraced as its natural end real science's opposite, natural end: moral and intellectual vice (including foolishness and the chief natural end of foolishness: human misery).

Since the time of Descartes, 'science" falsely-so-called has divorced itself from any essential connection to wisdom, virtue—especially prudence—and human happiness, and a creator-God (from all human good); and has identified itself with an intellectually-blind urge (misnamed 'will') to power. Such being the case, having embraced a kind of intellectual Machiavellianism as its nature, why should anyone be surprised to discover such a blind urge eventually to reveal itself as the neo-sophistic inclination to dominate: naked violence, universal despotism?

Gilson maintained that, from time immemorial, we in the West have based our cultural creed and scientific inspiration upon the conviction that gods, or a God, existed. All of our Western intellectual and cultural institutions have presupposed the existence of a God or gods. No longer. All of a sudden, God no longer exists. Worse, He never existed! For Gilson, the implication is clear: "We shall have to change completely our every thought, word and deed. The entire human order totters on its base."

If our entire cultural history depended upon the unswerving conviction that God exists, "the totality of the future must needs depend on the contrary certitude that God does not exist." The metaphysical terror now becomes evident in its depths. Nietzsche's message is a metaphysical bomb more powerful than the atomic weapon dropped on Hiroshima: "Everything that was true from the beginning of the human race will suddenly become false."[56]

Moreover, mankind alone must create for itself a new self-definition, which will become human destiny, the human project: *To destroy.* To build the world anew, to create the new scientific world

---

[56] Gilson, *The Terrors of the Year 2000*, 28. I thank John N. Deely for reminding me that postmodernism as popularly understood today is essentially (1) modernism in its natural stage of maturity: decay; and (2) should properly be called 'postmodernism falsely-so-called.'

order, we must first destroy the old. The only rational justification that modern mathematical physics can give to be the sole repository of truth is a Machiavellian-like ability to torture nature to reveal secrets: to destroy. Gilson claimed Nietzsche knew that, as long as we believe that what is dead is alive, we can never use our creative liberty. Nietzsche knew and readily admitted his mission was to destroy.

If Nietzsche was speaking the truth about his project, which Gilson thought he was, Gilson maintained that he was announcing the dawn of a new age in which the aim of Nitezsche's misnamed 'post-modern' culture, its metaphysical project, is to make war upon, to overthrow, traditional truths and values. To build our brave, new, scientific world order, we have to overthrow the metaphysical and moral foundations of Western culture. "Before stating what will be true, we will have to say that everything by which man has thus far lived, everything by which he still lives, is deception and trickery." As Gilson claimed Nietszche understood, "He who would be a creator, both in good and evil, must first of all know how to destroy and to wreck values."[57]

In fact, Gilson stated, our traditional Western values are intentionally being wrecked all around us, everywhere, under our feet. He said he had stopped counting "the unheard of theories thrown at us under names as various as their methods of thought, each the harbinger of a new truth which promises to create shortly, joyously busy

---

[57] Gilson, *The Terrors of the Year 2000*, 21–25, 28–29.

preparing the brave new world of tomorrow by first of all annihilating the world of today."[58]

What, then, are we who oppose Nietzsche's project to do in the face of such a cataclysm? Nietzsche's plan, his mission, is to destroy "today to create tomorrow." Gilson considered forgivable that we should not have anticipated Nietzsche's advent. "But," he said, "that we should not understand what he is doing while he is doing it right under our eyes, just as we were told he would do it—that bears witness to a stranger blindness. Can it really be that the herd of human being that is led to the slaughter has eyes and yet does not see?" Gilson's explanation for such a depth of blindness was that the announcement of a catastrophe of such an order usually leaves us "but a single escape: to disbelieve it and, in order not to believe, to refuse to understand."[59]

Whether Gilson thought Maritain suffered from such blindness, I do not know. I think he did. At the very least, Gilson clearly appeared to be saying that, if a natural law truly exists, looking today to international law for evidence of its existence and the notion of the dignity of the person that supports it historically in order to overcome contemporary Babelism cannot work. The chief reason that our falsely-so-called 'postmodern' world is essentially hostile to such notions is rooted in the late modern world's essential moral, metaphysical, and political rejection of the first extrinsic principle of natural law: the existence of a creator-God.

---

[58] Gilson, *The Terrors of the Year 2000*, 16–18.
[59] Gilson, *The Terrors of the Year 2000*, 17.

Instead of presuming a common agreement about the existence of a natural law upon which to build a common consensus about human nature, Maritain would have been better off facing the reality of the world around him, in recognizing that the modern project is essentially rooted in a rejection of natures, or forms, in things and that Babelism in modern thought cannot be overcome unless and until, like an alcoholic incapable or self-recovery, modernity first hits bottom and accepts a common understanding that forms exist in facultatively-independent realities. If modernism and false postmodernism are built upon a rejection of the existence of forms in things and of gods, or a creator-God, upon which the classical understanding of natural law depends, how can we make appeals to that law to give us a true postmodernism based upon the common understanding of the human person that will allow for communication between substances?

Were he alive today, I have no doubt St. Thomas's answer to this question would be that we can do so by recalling that, properly understood, natural law is nothing other than the way human beings participate in divine prudence, and God's uncommon common sense.

According to St. Thomas is prudence simply a species of uncommon common sense in the sense that, in whatever individual and culture it first comes to exist, it does so by meditating on the behavior of people with practical and productive understanding (people with 'know-how' like farmers, sailors, businessmen, craftsmen) related to what causes different organizational wholes with which they are experientially familiar to behave the way they do in reality, in the individual situation.

St. Thomas tells us that, etymologically, the word 'prudence' is simply a contraction of the Latin term *'providentiai'* ('providence'—being able to 'see ahead', anticipate the implications of our actions). This is something fools can never do.

In addition, in what is often referred to as his famous 'Treatise on Law' (*Summa theologiae*, 1a2ae, qq. 90–97), Thomas maintains that the natural law is simply God's divine providence (prudence) as this applies to moral choices we human beings make.

By following prudence in our moral choices, we human beings do nothing other than measure our behavior to conform to God's prudence as contained within natural law as this applies generically, specifically, and individually to us living our daily lives as rational animals—not as beasts!

When we intentionally behave in conformity with properly understood principles of natural law, we do more than follow brute, animal instinct. Through a healthy conscience, we conform our behavior to the rule of eternal, divine and human law as principles of human action that exist within reality—the providential order—as real measures of divine prudence given to members of the human species by a providential God!

In its healthy form, conscience connects human beings to natural law, divine prudence, and sense reality in the individual situation. In so doing it: (1) stands as an obstacle to us becoming madmen and (2) essentially enables us to possess beautiful human souls through which we might achieve fully human perfection and live a beautiful human life in all respects in this life and the next.

Chapter 2

Mortimer J. Adler on Universal Principles of Education

As the title of this presentation clearly indicates, I take as my point of departure for this meditation an essay written close to 80 years ago (in 1941) by the great American educator Mortimer J. Adler entitled, "Are There any Universal Principles on Which Education Should Be Founded?"[1]

Toward the start of this article, Adler claims that, like medicine (which he calls, "the art of using knowledge about the body to prevent and cure disease, to sustain and improve health"), education is a practical activity. Just as medicine is the art of using knowledge about the body to prevent and cure disease, to sustain and improve health, "so education is an art of using knowledge about the nature of man" (by which Adler means, about a human being, whether male or female) as an organizational whole comprised of organi-

---

[1] Mortimer J. Adler, "Are There any Universal Principles on Which Education Should Be Founded?", in Mortimer J. Adler, *Reforming Education: The Opening of the American Mind*, ed. Geraldine Van Doren (New York: Macmillan Publishing Company and London: Collier Macmillan Publishers, 1988), 56–65. This essay first appeared in the Philosophcial Journal *Studia Gilsoniana* 9, no. 4 (October–December 2020): 651–661. I thank the current editor, Imelda Chłodna Błach to reprint a revised and updated version in this current volume of mine.

zational parts that harmonize to generate human action) "to prevent and cure ignorance to sustain and improve what one might call mental or spiritual health."[2]

Such being the case, because whatever any human being's goals are, they are, for him or her, foundational educational principles, Adler maintains that "the educational principles that generate educational policy should be the ends aimed at "by anyone undertaking any educational responsibilities for himself or others."[3]

Nonetheless, Adler maintains, "The ends of education, the ends men should seek, are always and everywhere the same. They are absolute in the same sense that they are not relative to time and place, to individual differences and the variety of cultures. There are universal in the sense that they are invariable and without exception."[4]

The chief reason for this is, as Adler explains, many philosophies of education among which we can choose according to our tastes and temperaments do not exist. Just as we human beings must accept as essential first principles of doing natural science the well-establish rules of natural science "according to the weight of

---

[2] Adler, "Are There any Universal Principles on Which Education Should Be Founded?", 56.

[3] Adler, "Are There any Universal Principles on Which Education Should Be Founded?", 57.

[4] Adler, "Are There any Universal Principles on Which Education Should Be Founded?", 57.

the evidence and the dictates of reason," so, Adler claims, we must apply the same principles toward educational policy.[5]

In defense of his forceful assertion that *only one true educational philosophy exists* Adler offers three propositions: that human nature is: (1) everywhere the same; (2) something not fully, perfectly, developed at birth; and (3) the ends of education are twofold: proximate and ultimate.[6]

Elaborating on his first proposition, Adler states:

"My first and basic proposition is that human nature is everywhere the same. The universality and constancy of human nature, the same throughout history, the same in various cultures, the same in different individuals, is the source of the universal and absolute principles of education." Once again, by human "nature" Adler means a specific cause intrinsically existing within each and every human being that inclines its parts harmoniously to organize to generate specifically-one, chief action, like all the parts of a symphony orchestra harmonize to generate symphonic music, not fighting fires or playing "rock and roll." Hence, he adds, "By human nature I mean the nature of the human offspring has at birth—whatever it is that makes that all offspring something capable of growing into a man rather than the flea or a pig."

To this clarification, he emphasizes an essential property that "all human offspring have is potentialities or capacities for growth

---

[5] Adler, "Are There any Universal Principles on Which Education Should Be Founded?", 57.

[6] Adler, "Are There any Universal Principles on Which Education Should Be Founded?", 58–59.

and development." His point in saying this "is simply that the offspring of papa and mama flea, papa and mama pig, does not have the capacity for becoming a man. Trying to make a baby pig into a man is one miracle no educator has ever attempted, though some have tried and almost succeeded, in making a man-child into an adult pig."[7]

Consequently, when Adler talks about "the constancy and universality of human nature," he means "precisely what a biologist means when he speaks of the uniformity in procreation of any animal or plant species." Whether or not a human species as a composite, organizational, whole has *evolved* from other species or other species have evolved from it, is irrelevant to the issue at hand. "So long as the human species endures on earth," Adler states, "all members of that species will have the same specific nature, and it is the same specific nature which I say is everywhere the same."[8] That is, so long as specific human nature exists as the organizational whole that its parts essentially and harmoniously generate (so long as a symphony orchestra is a symphony orchestra, for example), it is everywhere specifically identical.

Regarding his second proposition, Adler asserts that this "is the definition of education itself." As Adler has described it, specific human nature existing within individual human beings, is an

---

[7] Adler, "Are There any Universal Principles on Which Education Should Be Founded?", 58–59.

[8] Adler, "Are There any Universal Principles on Which Education Should Be Founded?", 58.

imperfectly-developed organizational, causal whole, an organizational whole that is not fully, maturely, perfectly existing at birth. Specific human nature only exists within individual human natures, is an essential cause uniting them into the same genus of rational animal. At birth, our specific nature causes us to come into existence as unequally developed in our natural powers and abilities, capacities, as an organizational whole. As we live, if properly exercised, our human powers, abilities, and organiza-tional activities maturely develop, become increasingly qualitatively more perfect.

Precisely because, at birth, all individual human beings have limited natural (organizational) abilities, capacities, to grow in strength, mature, Adler claims, "Education is the process whereby a man helps himself or another to become what he can be."[9]

As just stated, Adler adds that his definition is not complete. We human beings can change for better or worse, to be a better or worse human beings. Hence, the specific difference of education properly understood must maintain it to be "the process whereby a man is changed for the better, whereby a man helps himself or another to become a good man, which is something he can be, though perhaps not as readily as being a bad man."

Adler then gives two reasons why education must be a process for human betterment, not for human corruption—(1) because education is everywhere and always recorded as a process of human improvement. For a person to ask why education must be for

---

[9] Adler, "Are There any Universal Principles on Which Education Should Be Founded?", 61.

human betterment and not human corruption, he asserts, "is like asking why medical therapy aims at restoring or improving health rather than at spreading disease"; and (2) because, if education were not, in fact, for human betterment, Adler asks, how could contemporary educators "justify compulsory educa-tion?"

The fact that contemporary, professional educators all tend to "approve, as just and wise, the laws requiring every potential citizen to submit to a certain minimum of education," and the fact that most of them "would like to increase that minimum a great deal, indicate" to Adler that professional educators think that "education is good for men (just as we think health is good for them, and still make certain hygienic observances compulsory)."[10]

Regarding his third basic proposition, Adler states that it logically follows from his first two.

"In light of the constancy and universality of specific nature, especially as a set of capacities for development, and in light of the definition of education as a process of developing those capacities to the best realization," Adler states, he is able to "say that the ends of education are twofold: proximate an ultimate. The proximate ends of education are the moral and intellectual virtues. ... The ultimate end of education is happiness or a good human life, life enriched by the possession of every kind of good, by the enjoyment of every type of satisfaction."

He then presents his reason for this distinction between the proximate ends and the ultimate end of education. Even though

---

[10] **Adler**, "Are There any Universal Principles on Which Education Should Be Founded?", 61–62.

they are indispensable, more than good habits are required for happiness: "The educator is as educator not responsible for providing all the conditions indispensable to happiness, but only some, and those are the virtues, or good habits. That is why we speak of the virtues or good habits as the proximate ends of education, and we mention happiness as the ultimate end because it would be wrong to suppose that the virtues were ends in themselves—they are ends, but they are also means–means to happiness."

Adler then identifies the intellectual and moral virtues as the proximate ends of education, good habits of knowing and thinking being the intellectual virtues; and good habits of desiring and freely acting being the moral virtues.[11]

Having done this, he states:

"If specific human nature is everywhere and at all times the same in all men, then all men have the same powers or capacities to be developed—though, as individuals, they differ in the degree or extent to which they possess these capacities.

"If the powers or capacities just referred to are parts of human nature, they are natural capacities, and as natural each has a nature—a determinate character, by which he tends naturally toward a certain kind of development.

---

[11] Adler, "Are There any Universal Principles on Which Education Should Be Founded?", 60.

"Therefore, habits, as developments of powers or fulfillment of capacities, can be said to be good if they conform to the natural tendency of the power or capacity which they develop."[12]

For example, Adler maintains:

"The power of knowing, shared by all men, is perfected by habits of knowledge, not by habits of error or by that privation of knowledge which we called ignorance. Similarly, the power of thinking shared by all men is perfected by habits of thinking well, by the arts of thinking; it is not perfected, but rather wasted or ruined, by habits of thinking poorly or inartistically.

Hence I say that we call a habit good when it perfects a power, when it develops the capacity in the direction toward which that capacity naturally tends."[13]

In light of his preceding argument, and because our specific nature and natural capacities are specifically the same, Adler concludes that the intellectual and moral virtues and the chief aim they naturally incline to generate (human happiness) are specifically the same for all human beings.

His proof thus having been completed to his satisfaction, Adler summarizes it thus: "If education must aim at the betterment of men by forming good habits in them, and if the virtues, or good habits, are the same for all men because their natural capacities are

---

[12] Adler, "Are There any Universal Principles on Which Education Should Be Founded?", 61.

[13] Adler, "Are There any Universal Principles on Which Education Should Be Founded?", 61.

the same and tend naturally to the same developments, then it follows that the virtues, or good habits, as the ends of education, are the absolute and universal principles on which education should be founded."[14]

He then immediately adds that his "conclusion follows logically: "but it is true only if the premises—the two *ifs* are true."

He then claims, "The truth of these two premises is guaranteed by two propositions which I think cannot be denied by anyone: my first proposition about the constancy of specific human nature, and my second proposition, i. e., the definition of education as a process of betterment."[15]

And he maintains that if his premises are true and his reasoning is valid, his conclusion is inescapably true.[16]

According to Adler, for a person who professes to be an 'educator' to disagree with his argument, that person would have to deny the reality of all intellectual and moral virtue: for example, the intellectual virtues traditionally known as "the liberal arts," the possession of which better the individual human intellect and make one individual human intellect better than another; the reality of the liberal arts of logic, sound reasoning, and grammar: which contains linguistic rules for distinguishing between meaningful and meaningless utterances.

---

[14] **Adler**, "Are There any Universal Principles on Which Education Should Be Founded?", 61.

[15] **Adler**, "Are There any Universal Principles on Which Education Should Be Founded?", 61–62.

[16] **Adler**, "Are There any Universal Principles on Which Education Should Be Founded?", 62.

More than this. Adler maintains that rejection of his argument would require an 'educator' to deny as an educational responsibility the existence of the moral "virtue of justice, a justice that is the same for all men everywhere, which should always be the aim of moral education to cultivate." If just forms of government are naturally good for a human being, naturally better than unjust, totalitarian, ones, Adler maintains, "Any educational system which trains men to be just in their dealings with other men is objectively better than one which prepares some men for slavery and others to use them as their tools."

To conclude, Adler claims that legitimate educators must agree with him that some intellectual and moral virtues exist the same for all men everywhere that always are the natural ends of education. If they choose to disagree with him they must: (1) "make no appeals whatsoever to logic and grammar as canons of sound thinking and correct speech"; be willing to (2) violate the intellectual principle of non-contradiction; and (3) claim that "there is no such thing as justice, that there is nothing wrong with tyranny and slavery, with medieval inquisitions or modern gestapos, and that anyone who says democracy is the best form of government is talking through his hat."

Having laid his cards on the table, Adler invites those who disagree with him to do the same.[17]

Having done so, however, I think Adler has made a serious error of not showing all his cards. For, as anyone, like Adler, who

---

[17] **Adler**, "Are There any Universal Principles on Which Education Should Be Founded?", 62–65.

has studied the teachings of Aristotle knows, Adler's entire argument rests upon the existence of natural human powers, capacities, habits existing as properties caused by the existence of an intellectual soul, on human beings being essentially rational animals, hylomorphic-composite-whole-organizations of soul and body. Such being the case, to agree with Adler, contemporary educators would have to admit the existence of a human soul in which human faculties, powers, habits exist; and also the reality of ends, aims, in really-existing natures.

Moreover, because specific human nature and its essential properties, powers, and abilities are unequally possessed by individual human beings, contemporary, 'Enlightened' educators would have to admit the existence not only of commutative justice, but also of contributive and distributive justice. Such admissions as the existence of a human, or any, nature; an intellectual soul; the reality of aims, ends, in things; and contributive and distributive justice essentially contradict the foundational principles of the Enlightenment understanding of reality and human beings. The Enlightenment considers human beings to be systems of feelings; real natures and real aims not to exist; and justice to be determined by the sincere feelings of Enlightened emotional elites. "Enlightened philosophy of education" falsely-so-called is a caricature of real human education that Adler has brilliantly exposed for what it is. Shame that he folded his hand prematurely and did not take full advantage of exposing it to be the total fraud it is.

Chapter 3

The Essential Connection between Commonsense Philosophy and Leadership Excellence[1]

I take as my point of departure for this paper two claims I made in my opening talk at the 2014 July international congress on "Renewing the West by Renewing Common Sense" in Huntington, Long Island, NY, USA:

(1) *'An art or science grows out of a human habit to which a subject known relates, that the subject known helps generate and activate within a natural human knowing faculty."*

(2) *"Every art, science, or philosophical activity grows out of the experiential relationship between the specific habit of an artist, scientist, or philosopher and a known material or subject that activates the habit."*

---

[1] This paper somewhat amends and expands slightly on the talk entitled "The Essential Connection between Commonsense Philosophy and Leadership Excellence," which I presented at the *Inaugural International Congress, Renewing the West by Renewing Common Sense*, 17 to 20 July 2014, at Immaculate Conception Seminary, Huntington, Long Island, NY, USA. My talk was given in Plenary Session 7 on 18 July 2014. This essay first appeared in the Philosophcial Journal *Studia Gilsoniana* 3:supplement (2014): 605–617 | ISSN 2300–0066. I thank the current editor, Imelda Chłodna Błach to reprint a revised and updated version in this current volume of mine.

"Eliminate one of the essential parts of this relationship," I said, "and the activity can no longer exist. No such subject (such as somewhat sickly bodies) known, or no habit of medicine in a physician, no art of medicine. The relation between the artist or scientist and the artistic or scientific subject known generates the habit and act of art and science. The two are essentially connected. Eliminate one or the other extreme of the relationship and the artistic, scientific, or philosophical activity becomes destroyed."[2] We take the nature, divisions, and methods, of all experience, art, philosophy/science, and leadership, from an essential relationship between human habits existing within human faculties and a known material, or known subject, that activates these human abilities.

As I think most people familiar with any of the human qualities of experience, art, science/philosophy, or leadership implicitly, if not explicitly, realize (at least in our saner, common sense, moments), all these human principles chiefly grow out of an essential relationship among the human intellect, will, and emotions and an organizationally and operationally deprived body (an incompletely developed organizational and operational whole, one that can be receptive to or resist further organizational and operational development, or improvement) and a chief action that parts of that

---

[2] Peter A. Redpath, Plenary Session 3 Address (17 July 2014), "The Nature of Common Sense and How We use Common Sense to Renew the West," *Inaugural International Congress, Renewing the West by Renewing Common Sense*, 17 to 20 July 2014.

Chapter 3: The Essential Connection   79

deprived body naturally and cooperatively incline to produce, or aim (end) they incline to realize.

The first beginnings of my explicit realization of this reality came to me decades ago while I was reading Book 1 of Plato's *Republic*, in which Socrates gives Polemarchos examples of people ancient Athenians reasonably considered to be artists: cooks, physicians, pilots of ships, money makers, traders, and so on. In each case, Socrates made evident to Polemarchos that, to be an artist, a person has to work with some kind of essentially improvable body; that an artistic subject, body, or organization that the artist, in some way, improves has to be essentially deprived, impoverished, but improvable.[3]

Subsequent reading of different works of Armand A. Maurer showing that St. Thomas understood (1) the genus, or subject, of the philosopher to be essentially different from the genus of the logician; (2) philosophy to be chiefly an intellectual habit, not a body of knowledge;[4] and (3) analogy to be "above all . . . a doctrine

---

[3] Plato, *Republic*, Bk. 1, 331D–334B.

[4] Armand A. Maurer, "The Unity of a Science: St. Thomas and the Nominalists," in *St. Thomas Aquinas, 1274–1974, Commemorative Studies*. 2 vols. Toronto: Pontifical Institute of Mediaeval Studies, 1974), vol. 2, 269–291. See, also, Maurer, "Introduction," in *St. Thomas Aquinas, The Divisions and Methods of the Sciences, Questions V and VI of his Commentary on the de Trinitate of Boethius*, trans. with an intro. and notes Armand A. Maurer (Toronto: Pontifical Institute of Mediaeval Studies, 3rd rev. ed., 1963), 75, fn. 15. See. St. Thomas Aquinas, *In I Sent.*

of a *judgment* of analogy or proportion rather than an analogous *concept*" caused me to start to realize that none of the leading twentieth-century students of St. Thomas, including Jacques Maritain and Étienne Gilson, had adequately understood his teaching about many of his most fundamental principles, including his understanding of philosophy and science.[5] At that point, I decided that I had better start to investigate these issues on my own.

Spending many years studying these matters, among other things, this is what I discovered. For St. Thomas Aquinas, philosophy, science, is, just as for Aristotle before him, chiefly an intellectually-virtuous, habitual knowledge born of sense wonder. This philosophical, scientific, wonder is essentially about a multitude of beings already known to be one or a whole and the memory of the way an individual has been able to acquire much memory of this multitude as one or a whole.

Just as a human being cannot become morally virtuous without practice, habitually choosing what is right in the right way, no human being can become intellectually virtuous (scientific, philosophical) without much practice, habitually judging about what he

---

d. 19, q. 5, a. 2, ad 1; *Commentary on the Metaphysics of Aristotle*, lect. 12, nn. 2142–2144; and *Summa theologiae*, 1, 66, 2, ad 2 and 88, 2, ad 4.

[5] Armand A. Maurer, *The Philosophy of William of Ockham in Light of its Principles* (Toronto: Pontifical Institute of Mediaeval Studies, 1999), 278.

Chapter 3: The Essential Connection

or she has already rightly conceived and judged, habitually engaging in right reasoning about already existing orders of truths, things known.

More precisely, according to St. Thomas, all philosophy, science, starts in sense wonder essentially involving a complicated psychological state of *fear*, intellectual confidence about the unity of truth and the essential reliability of our sense and intellectual faculties, personal *hope* to achieve intellectual, volitional, and emotional satisfaction though resolving the wonder and putting the fear to rest.

As St. Thomas recognized even before the historical birth of some later, mistaken notions of philosophy's first principle of generation, philosophy does not start in faith seeking understanding, absolute skepticism, universal method doubt, impossible dreams of pure reason, Absolute Spirit's urge to emerge, veils of ignorance, or any of the other starting points that Western intellectuals, mistaking themselves to be doing philosophy, have proposed over the centuries. *It starts in an opposition between fear and hope in which the act of philosophizing, pursuing science, essentially constitutes an act of hope of success based upon an essential conviction about the unity of truth and the essential reliability of our human sense and intellectual faculties.*

St. Thomas maintained that wonder is a species of fear that results from ignorance of a cause.[6] Because the formal object of fear

---

[6] St. Thomas Aquinas, *Summa theologiae*, 1–2, 44, 4, ad 5.

calls to mind a difficulty of some magnitude and a sense of dissatisfying personal weakness (an immediate sense of opposition, dependency, and privation), the desire to philosophize, engage in science, can only arise within a person who can experience a complicated psychological state involving a natural desire to escape from the fear we experience of the real difficulty, danger, and damage ignorance can cause us; *personal self-confidence* that our sense and intellectual faculties are reliable enough to help us put this fear to rest by knowing about the truth of things as expressed in the truth of our intellectual and sensory judgments, and some *hope* in our personal ability to use our intellectual and sense faculties to put this fear to rest by rationally resolving an apparently irreconcilable contradiction; and, by so doing, achieving a state of intellectual, volitional, and emotional satisfaction that we have done so.

St. Thomas explained that this initial sense of fear grips us in two stages: (1) recognition of our intellectual weakness and fear of failure causes us to refrain immediately from passing judgment; and (2) *hope* of possibility of understanding an effect's cause prompts us intellectually to seek the cause.[7]

---

[7] Aquinas, *Summa theologiae*, 1–2, 44, 4, ad 5; and St. Thomas Aquinas, *Commentary on the Metaphysics of Aristotle*, Bk. 1, lect. 3 and *Summa theologiae*, qq. 40 and 41 dealing with hope and fear. My analysis of St. Thomas's teaching about the nature of philosophy and the relation of sense wonder to philosophy/science is based upon St. Thomas's explicit teaching about wonder and the emotions of fear and hope as contrary opposites. I have pieced it together from the teachings St. Thomas

Chapter 3: The Essential Connection

Actually, this fear appears to include an intervening third stage between fear and hope in which we experience intellectual, volitional, and emotional dissatisfaction with being in a state of fear and a determination to eliminate it. Thomas added that, since philosophical investigation starts with wonder, it must end in the contrary of wonder (a species of fear), in some sort of satisfaction that puts fear to rest.

St. Thomas recognized that we do not, and cannot, wonder about the answer to questions we already know, about what is evident, or about what we consider *impossible* to know; and, strictly speaking, when working as philosophers, scientists, we do not seek to remain in a state of wonder.[8]

We seek to put wonder to rest by discovering the causes that have generated the wonder. Since wonder is the first principle of all theoretical, practical, or productive philosophy, science, for everyone and all time, initially all philosophical first principles arise from our common sense pre-philosophical, pre-scientific knowledge, human senses, emotions, intellect, will, personal self-confidence about the reliability of our sense and intellectual faculties and the unity of truth as expressed in things and in the human intellect, and something that causes in us the awareness of real opposition, possession and privation (not simply difference).

---

gives about the emotions of fear and hope and the nature of sense wonder.

[8] St. Thomas Aquinas, *Commentary on the Metaphysics of Aristotle*, Bk. 1, lect. 3.

Consequently, since, in its nature and origin philosophy, science, presupposes knowledge of the existence of several things and complicated psychological states, including something we fear can hurt us, and the hope of overcoming this fear, the mental attitude of complete skepticism is a contradictory opposite, and cannot simultaneously co-exist with, the mental state of philosophy.

No matter what modern confidence men like René Descartes and his historical descendants, posing as philosophers and scientists, tell us, philosophy, science, cannot pre-exist knowledge. Philosophy, science, presupposes knowledge, including common sense knowledge of evident truths, and is born of sense wonder. People who cannot wonder cannot become philosophers, scientists. And people who think they have the one philosophical method finally to put all wonder to rest are delusional. Only God has the one method to put all wonder to rest.

Since only people who fear ignorance wonder about how to escape from it, strictly speaking, none of us is a born a philosopher or scientist; seeking to become a philosopher, scientist, is not something that all human beings explicitly desire to do; and engaging in philosophical, scientific, reasoning is not something all human beings do, can do, or even want to do.

People who are content to be in a state of ignorance cannot become philosophers, scientists. As Plato and Socrates emphasized, people cannot pour philosophy, science, into us like inserting vision into blind eyes.[9] Only those who have some knowledge and experience of this initial sort of fear, accompanied by the appropriate desire to put it to rest, can become philosophers, scientists.

For this reason, absolute skeptics cannot become philosophers, cannot even start the journey to become philosophers. Hence, when Socrates confronted people who were content to be ignorant, he attempted to jolt them out of their blissful ignorance by publicly shaming them, by driving them through Socratic irony into an *aporia* (an intellectual dead end), into becoming aware of the dangers of their ignorance.

Aside from the first principle of sense wonder, then, philosophy's, science's, specific, or *proximate*, common sense first principles include: (1) habits of knowing faculties; (2) existing things, real natures; (3) prior knowledge of these existing things; (4) the existence and knowledge of fear, hope; (5) desire to escape from fear and possess hope; (6) convictions of certainty about the: (a) unity of truth; (b) reliability of human sense and intellectual faculties; (c) and the existence and knowledge of real opposites.

Since philosophy's, science's, first principles include human knowing faculties, since sense wonder must exist in sense wonderers, the existence of philosophy, science (at least a common sense

---

[9] Plato, *Republic*, Bk. 7, 518B–518D.

philosophy and science) essentially depends upon an understanding of human nature that involves human beings possessed of a human soul (or some identical, if differently named, psychological principle) that can generate human knowing faculties that can possess human habits.

Since denial of the existence of a faculty psychology involves essential denial of one of philosophy's essential principles of wonder (the wonderer), no human being can rationally, or with common sense, affirm the existence of philosophy/science and simultaneously deny the existence of the only human knowing principle capable of essentially producing philosophical/scientific activity: human knowing faculties.

Leading ancient Greek philosophers considered (1) philosophy and science to be identical and (2) the generic subject that all philosophy, science (not just physics) studies to be the problem of the one and the many.[10] Aristotle, especially, considered the subject of a science to consist of two main parts: (1) one genus (many hierarchically-ordered species related to one nature: *an operational organization* [an organization equipped with all the parts needed to operate organizationally]); unequal possession of one nature by a multitude of species [parts]) united to each other as parts by means of a common, and unequal, relationship of each to some whole nature (the organization) through the relationship of

---

[10] I have extensively and rigorously defended this claim in my book *Wisdom's Odyssey from Philosophy to Transcendental Sophistry* (Amsterdam and Atlanta: Editions Rodopi B.V.: 1997).

a topmost part to a chief aim, or universal act (similar to the way a commanding general unites all of the parts of one army together to each other and to the whole army through a chief aim of military victory); (2) an intellectual habit, or virtue, that consists of ordering many acts of imagining, conceiving, judging, and reasoning to arrive at some evident, concluding judgment: a scientific conclusion arrived at through deductive reasoning, or demonstration.[11]

For Aristotle science is not chiefly a system, and it does not solely consist in a scientific demonstration. Scientific demonstration culminates scientific understanding like a crescendo culminates a symphonic musical performance. Science is chiefly a generic habit of knowing (of right judging about definitions, concepts, images, and sensible and non-sensible natures [operational organizations]). Science chiefly exists in the scientist's distinctive and comprehensive (that is, *generic*) habit of sensing, abstracting, imagining, conceiving, and judging; but chiefly in judging: in relation to the way a scientist is inclined by habit to abstract and relate concepts and images in a unique act of judging, reasoning, and drawing conclusions (species of the scientist's generic habit).

This is a *comprehensive understanding* (a scientific explanation) *that*, as history of philosophical experience has taught us, to

---

[11] Aquinas, *Commentary on the Metaphysics of Aristotle*, Bk. 1, nn. 18–35; Bk. 3, l. 1 through l. 12; *Commentary on the Nicomachean Ethics of Aristotle*, Bk. 2, l. 1, n. 246; Bk. 6, l. 3; *Posterior Analytics*, Bk 1, l. 10 through 21.

be completely sure of being scientific, *culminates in a demonstration and a process of verification that demonstrative knowledge is possessed through testing what a scientist considers to be demonstrative knowledge in the form of a confirmed hypothesis* (somewhat like editing the final draft of a book for typographical errors).

Strictly speaking, considered in and of itself, a demonstrative syllogism or system of demonstrative syllogisms is, no scientific, no philosophical, no scientific, explanation.

Precisely speaking, *a philosophical or scientific explanation is communication of a knowledge of necessary whole/part relations through single act of understanding* given by one person to himself or herself, or to another person, of how parts essentially unite to form a whole or how a whole is divided into parts. I call this a "comprehensive understanding": a single, or generic, act of understanding that ties together all the parts of an investigation into a whole in a Eureka moment that culminates in a demonstrative conclusion that is verified by final testing of the prior reasoning process!

Strictly speaking, *all explanations, including all scientific, philosophical, ones, are personally-caused acts of recollected knowing unified into a single, whole (one generic act of understanding) communicated to oneself or another.* Science is chiefly a psychological act, an act of the human soul, or, better, the human person: a personally-caused act of comprehensive understanding.

Like Aristotle says, art and science, philosophy, presuppose experience, or much memory *habitually related to judging* that some multitude is essentially related as 1: as parts to a whole (that is, as species [organizational parts] to a genus, or organizational whole).

The reason for this is that art and science (the latter being, strictly speaking, identical with philosophy for Aristotle and St. Thomas) are reflections upon experience, upon prior knowledge that produces a memory—indeed, much memory that helps, through practice, to produce experience and a universal judgment about cause/effect relations. For example, medical experience grows out of much memory (much knowledge) that when given a specific medicine in specific dosages at specific times a person recovers from an illness.

Because it studies much memory related as a one, or whole, to parts of a scientific subject, the philosophical, scientific, habit can *analogously* be called a 'system,' or 'body of knowledge'; but such way of talking is imprecise, and if used as a starting point for developing philosophical, scientific, understanding of St. Thomas's teaching, can lead to major mistakes down the road. Better to say it is chiefly an intellectual habit that studies systems or a single genus divided by extremes, or contrary opposites.

Every science studies many things, but only a limited number of them. The unity of a science comes from the unity of the multitude a scientist studies (a genus or operational organization) as related to a chief (or one main, generic) habit possessed by the mind of the scientist related to a chief scientific interest or aim.

The limited multitude (genus: hierarchically-ordered species) that a science studies is established by extremes of privation and possession within the relationship of one whole (a nature) to many parts. For example, the science of medicine studies extremes of one generic nature, health, as health is most- and least-fully possessed by a multitude of bodily organs, and anything essentially related to achieving or maintaining health (like exercise, diet, books, medical instruments, and so on).[12]

Hence, the one science (generic habit of mind) of medicine studies extremes of health, opposites: health and disease (extreme species). The science, in turn, consists in the single, comprehensive, relationship between the knower and the things known established through this single, comprehensive, or generic habit of mind, ordering essential relationships among a multitude of specific habits of the respective science one to another in relation to the chief aim of the science considered as a generic habit.

Within each science, in turn, a most difficult set of chief questions, or problems, exists that a few persons can, through the excellence of their mental habit, solve better than anyone else. We rightly call such people 'wise' in that science.

Today, the unity of philosophy, science, and wisdom as St. Thomas understood it, can be re-established by recovering a proper understanding of science as chiefly an act of a scientific habit of a human soul. More than anything else, through distinctive habits of the human soul essentially related to known natures

---

[12] Aquinas, *Commentary on the Metaphysics of Aristotle*, Bk. 10.

Chapter 3: The Essential Connection 91

(organizational wholes made up of parts), human beings (not logical systems, premises, or ideas divorced from knowing habits) generate, cause, science. This is chiefly what makes the act of science praiseworthy; not the fact that a person has memorized a multitude of facts or can deduce factual conclusions from factual premises.

No human beings with comprehensive knowing habits, no science. No science, no happiness. The human soul is a chief, essential, and proximate cause of science. The soul produces the intellectual virtue of science. The intellectual virtue of science causes wisdom. And wisdom causes happiness.

Hence, being wrong about the nature of human science, condemns a person, culture, or civilization to human misery. This is precisely what is happening within Western civilization today.

Turning now to the issue of leadership, just as, according to St. Thomas, and Socrates, Plato, and Aristotle before him, the knower and the thing known constitute essential parts of the same genus, or organizational whole, so do leadership and the thing led. Because leadership is a kind of directing activity, and in human beings, in its highest form, is not a chance event, because human reason is its chief directing faculty, human leadership is a kind of knowing. Moreover, in its highest form, human leadership consists in a kind of philosophical/scientific way of knowing.

As a kind of knowing, leadership is chiefly a specific organizational habit existing within the highest part of organizational knowers, through which a leader is able, better than any other organizational part, to communicate a chief organizational aim to the other parts of an organization. Leadership, in short, is a chiefly a communications activity: an ability to communicate (in a way that need not be verbal or totally rational) specific superiority, exceeding other organizational parts in organizational strength, through which a leader is able to convey to, and elicit from, those led (other parts of an organization), receptivity to taking directions essentially related to the chief aim of an organization as an organization.

Obviously, the leader and the beings led belong to the same organization, or real genus. Leadership is not an abstraction. It is an essential part of a real relation. As a knowing activity, the leader belongs to the same organizational whole, or genus, that the leader leads. Fire chiefs belong to real fire departments, police chiefs to real police departments, and so on. Abstractly considered, leaders as leaders do not exist.

Nor does an art or science of anything as a real generic whole exist apart from its real species. Arts and sciences exist in and through their real species. Hence, the art of medicine as a genus did not come into existence and then the art of curing this or that disease. The art of curing this or that disease first came into existence, imperfectly encompassing the entire genus of medicine.

Strictly considered, experience, art, philosophy, science are not bodies of generically new knowledge added to something a leader

Chapter 3: The Essential Connection

already knows. They are more or less perfect, or maturely developed, habits, ways of possessing knowledge, understanding, a leader already has about some operational, organizational whole a leader leads.

Experienced leaders grow out of knowledgeable leaders familiar with the organizational composition of essentially different, necessary, part/whole relationships. The art of leadership essentially grows out of the experienced leadership of different organizational parts (leaders) knowing the essential and necessary operational relationships that, to operate harmoniously, these or those parts must have to each other and to a chief organizational aim. The philosophy or science of leadership essentially grows out of the art of leadership of different organizational parts knowing the organizational principles that guide organizational operational principles in relation to a chief organizational aim.

Put more simply in contemporary business and military terms, experienced leaders know that this or that needs to be done at this or that time, under this or that circumstance or condition, and can overcome resistance and induce receptivity when necessary to do what needs to be done when it needs to be done. Beyond experiential knowledge, someone who possesses knowledge through an artistic quality of soul resembles a person with the habit of mathematics who has memorized formulas and knows when they can reasonably be applied to solve this or that problem. Similarly, people with the art of leadership know the operational principles at work that cause doing this or that at this or that time, under this or that condition or circumstance, reasonable in relation to a tactical plan of operation. People possessed of the philosophy or science of leadership, however, more perfectly possess what they already know by apprehending it in relation to the strategic, or generic, plan and aim articulated in an organizational mission statement that generates the operational principles behind tactical operations in the here and now.

Such people know how to build and preserve organizations, have the qualities of great discoverers, pioneers, and great teachers. Because such people must constantly instill hope, drive out fear, build and restore confidence, energize and calm emotions, communicate a superior ability to know and unify potentially opposing convictions among free and intelligent agents about the right direction to take within an organizational operation to satisfy the chief organizational aim, such people must, best of all, know the first reason why this or that action needs to be done, how to do it, and, through emotional and volitional strength and resolve, be able to communicate this to themselves and others. As a result, such people can never be absolute skeptics, egalitarians, totalitarians, or anarchists.

In the process of gaining this philosophical, scientific, more perfect and complete, possession of their own leadership knowledge, along the way of being liberated from their prior intellectual weakness, knowingly or not, the best leaders have to become aided by the traditional seven liberal arts (the operational leadership qualities of human communication like grammar, rhetoric, logic; and arts that facilitate ways imagining the harmonic constitution of the physical universe, like arithmetic, geometry, astronomy, and music) *as well as the moral virtue of prudence and its handmaiden 'history,'* which renaissance humanists added to a new Western educational canon we now call the 'humanities.'

Despite claims to the contrary, none of these skills, any more than philosophy, consists in some esoteric teaching or body of knowledge that poets, rhetoricians, and, in modern times, mathematicians have claimed them to be. While, because it is no book, Galileo Galilei was wrong when he maintained that the book of nature is written in the language of mathematics, the physical universe is no body of facts or philosophy;[13] nor is it written in the language of mathematics, music, grammar, rhetoric, logic, poetry, the liberal arts as a whole, the Hegelian Absolute Spirit, the Marxist dialectic, egalitarianism, or libertarianism. If it were a book, it would be written in the language of organizational wholes, which is the way the ancient Greek philosophers understood it. Mathematics would be one of its chapters. And those capable of reading this book would be anyone with knowing habits capable of grasping the composite being of sensible things and wondering about it as an organizational whole.

---

[13] Galileo Galilei, *The Assayer*, trans. Stillman Drake, in *Discoveries and Opinions of Galileo*, ed. and trans. Stillman Drake (New York, Doubleday and Company, 1957), 237–238.

If we wish to renew the West, it is precisely to this understanding of common sense philosophy and leadership excellence that we need to return. I hope I have made evident to why this is so and that you will join me in this long-overdue, but essential, project.

Chapter 4

The Ideal of a University[1]

We meet today to start to plan a new renaissance in Western university education. In so doing, we engage in a historic moment. At such a time, we do well to recall Aristotle's sage admonition that a small mistake in the beginning multiplies later on and Étienne Gilson's prudent observation that we think the way we can, not the way we wish.[2] We meet to articulate practical principles based upon abstract considerations of the nature of a university. If the principles we derive are right, if we have precisely extracted them from the natures of things, not from unrealistic dreams or ungrounded imaginings, and if we and others in the future apply them prudently, with logical consistency, to the practical order, with a lot of good luck, or better, Divine guidance, what we plan to establish will be well-founded, flourish, and help to improve our culture.

---

[1] This essay is a slightly amended and expanded version of a paper that appeared close to 25 years ago in *Classical Homeschooling Magazine* (see: https://www.angelicum.net/classical-homeschooling-magazine/fourth-issue/the-ideal-of-a-university/. I thank the publisher Patrick S. J. Carmack for allowing me to republish and expand upon it here.

[2] Aristotle, *De caelo* (*On the Heavens*), Bk. 1, ch. 5, 27b8–13 and Étienne Gilson, *The Unity of Philosophical Experience* (New York: Charles Scribner's Sons, 1965), 302.

Failure to extract right principles from the being of things was the precise mistake made by the leading figures of the last three Western educational revolutions, Francesco Petrarcha (Petrarch), Réne Descartes, and Jean-Jacques Rousseau. Practical action never occurs within a vacuum. In practical matters, failure to understand our surroundings, the circumstances and conditions we need to generate an action, our context, involves an mistake of serious import. Petrarch, Descartes, and Rousseau made such a mistake.

In my opinion, Petrarch's revolution, which gave the Italian Renaissance its formal direction, started one day in Rome in 1341 when Petrarch was crowned poet laureate. The twentieth-century's leading historian of Renaissance thought, Paul Oskar Kristeller, describes this scene in a threefold way: (1) "The reading of the ancient Latin writers, and the sight of Rome's ancient monuments, evoked in Petrarch as in many other Italian humanists a strong nostalgia for the political greatness of the Roman Republic and Empire"; (2) "the hope to restore this greatness was the central political idea that guided" Petrarch in his dealings with the Pope and Emperor, with Cola di Rienzo, and with the various Italian governments"; and (3) Petrarch had the conviction that his coronation was a renewal in his person of "an ancient Roman honor."[3]

---

[3] Paul Oskar Kristeller, *Eight Philosophers of the Italian Renaissance* (Stanford: Stanford University Press, 1966), 7.

Chapter 4: The Ideal of a University

For our purposes, a main significance of these events is that the circumstances of Petrarch's time evoked in him a life work, a major goal. This was primarily a political, not an educational, project: to revive the greatness of the Roman Republic in a Christianized form. To do this Petrarch needed to change the direction of education. To do this, he had to revive an interest in reading pagan writers, especially rhetoricians and poets. To do this, he needed, in turn, to elevate the status of poets and rhetoricians in the university and within the eyes of the Church. To elevate this status, he took a commonly traveled road in the history of human thought: He sought to increase the status of the disciplines of poetry and rhetoric within the order of human learning and the eyes of Church authorities by decreasing and deconstructing other academic disciplines, especially some versions of scholastic theology.

By taking this road, wittingly or unwittingly, Petrarch did several things that, educationally, doomed his project to fail. He subordinated the goals of education to the goals of politics, something against which Plato wisely warns us in his discussion with Callicles in his dialogue the Gorgias.[4] By doing this, Petrarch: (1) made educational institutions instruments of, and subservient to, sophistry; (2) subordinated philosophy to rhetoric and poetry; (3) violated a metaphysical rule that Gilson says repeats itself in

---

[4] Plato, *Gorgias*, 481B–522E.

history: Philosophy always buries its undertakers;[5] and (4) revived academic disputes going back for centuries, to Plato's time and beyond.

During the Middle Ages these disputes had resurfaced between theologians and members of the faculty of arts in the monastic and cathedral schools, and among members of the faculty of arts, as the famed "battle of the arts."[6] This fight was a continuation of the age-old battle between philosophers and poets that Plato described in Book 10 of his famous Republic.[7]

For centuries, the Roman Catholic Church had not encouraged reading of pagan poets. In the Medieval trivium poetry was not even a separate division. The division was grammar, rhetoric, and logic. Because of extensive illiteracy during the Carolingian Renaissance, grammar and rhetoric played a more important role in the schools than did poetry. They tended to absorb poetry. After the eleventh century, poetry was taught within the liberal arts division of rhetoric as part of the art of letter

---

[5] Gilson, *The Unity of Philosophical Experience*, 306.

[6] Étienne Gilson, *History of Christian Philosophy in the Middle Ages* (New York: Random House), 1955, 312–316; Ralph M. McInerny, *A History of Western Philosophy: Philosophy from St. Augustine to Ockham*, vol. 2 (Notre Dame and London: University of Notre Dame Press, 1970), 161; and Ernst Robert Curtius, *European Literature and the Latin Middle Ages*, trans. Willard R. Trask (New York: Published by the Bollingen Foundation for Pantheon Books, 1952), 56, 77, 480–484.

[7] Plato, *Republic*, Bk. 10, 595A–607B.

writing [ars dictaminis]. Still, it was largely the Cinderella of the liberal arts.[8]

This brawl would erupt during the twelfth century as the Cornifician controversy at the cathedral School of Chartres and the monastery of St. Victor in Paris. At this time, the humanist John of Salisbury, William of Conches, and Hugh of St. Victor had gotten involved in a dispute related to the work of an unnamed author whom John of Salisbury had apparently dubbed Cornificius, "an opponent of Vergil."[9] The fight involved charges and counter-charges of heresy and watering down the school curriculum. John and others were especially concerned about the rise of the status of dialectics in the schools and monasteries, and the failure to read the "authors" or traditional "authorities."[10]

This dispute would spill over into the thirteenth century in Paris, where Henry of Andelys would describe it in his Battle of the Seven Liberal Arts. Petrarch would revive and redirect this dispute during the fourteenth century. As famed literary historian Ernest Robert Curtius rightly notes: "Between the world of John of

---

[8] Peter A. Redpath, *Wisdom's Odyssey from Philosophy to Transcendental Sophistry* (Amsterdam and Atlanta: Editions Rodopi, B.V., 1998), 50–56, 72–73, 93; Kristeller, *Eight Philosophers of the Italian Renaissance*, 150; Charles Trinkhaus, *In Our Image and Likeness: Humanity and Divinity in Italian Humanist Thought* (Chicago: The University of Chicago Press and London: Constable & Co. Ltd., 1970), vol. 2, 685.

[9] McInerny, *A History of Western Philosophy*, 161.

[10] Curtius, *European Literature and the Latin Middle Ages*, 52–53.

Salisbury and the world of Petrarch there is an intellectual kinship."[11]

Descartes's educational revolution is incomprehensible apart from understanding Petrarch's dream. Descartes's revolution is a moment in Petrarch's political project, a continuation of Petrarch's dream and of of the battle of the arts from a fight within the *trivium* to a battle between the *trivium* and the *quadrivium*.[12] In my opinion, because intellectuals within Western culture have failed accurately to locate Descartes's revolution within Western intellectual history, we find it difficult to extricate ourselves from the cultural mess into which we have fallen as a result of logical application of Cartesian and Enlightenment principles to our educational institutions.

Strictly speaking, Descartes was no philosopher, and the revolution he initiated was not philosophical. It was a humanist revolution, a continuation of the Battle of the Liberal Arts, most precisely among rhetoric, poetry, logic, and mathematics, going back through Descartes to Petrarch. Hence, in its roots, Descartes dream is an extension of Petrarch's dream, a political project designed to enhance Western culture by elevating logic and mathematics over all the other arts by reducing all the arts to them.

---

[11] Curtius, *European Literature and the Latin Middle Ages*, 77.

[12] For a more sustained argument of this position see my *Cartesian Nightmare: An Introduction to Transcendental Sophistry* (Amsterdam and Atlanta: Editions Rodopi, B.V., 1997).

Chapter 4: The Ideal of a University

Descartes got involved in this dispute because, centuries before him, to elevate the status of poetry and rhetoric over scholastic theology and philosophy, Petrarch had fabricated a story about the nature of philosophy that he had gotten through Medieval encyclopedists, like Cassiodorus and Isiodore. They, in turn, had gotten the story from St. Augustine, who had inherited it from Philo Judaeus through the teachings of St. Ambrose. According to this fabricated history, philosophy is a hidden teaching, an esoteric metaphysical and moral doctrine that Moses had initiated. Supposedly, according to the story, this teaching had been transmitted by Moses to posterity through Scripture and the work of pagan poets and philosophers, especially Plato and Vergil.[13]

By the end of the Renaissance, this fabricated tale about philosophy's origin had helped to elevate the status of poetry and rhetoric within many European universities and conflate theology with philosophy, and philosophy with poetry and rhetoric. It also stood as an obstacle to the development of mathematical science, especially within the schools of the Jesuits.[14]

This was the context in which we must understand the significance of the dream of Descartes to have discovered a wondrous system of science of clear and distinct ideas, buried in the hidden recesses of the mind. Descartes' revolution was primarily

---

[13] Redpath, *Cartesian Nightmare: An Introduction to Transcendental Sophistry*, 7–17. See also my *Wisdom's Odyssey*, 31–45.

[14] Redpath, *Wisdom's Odyssey*, 183–188 and *Cartesian Nightmare*, 19–20.

directed against Renaissance humanism and toward a new mathematicized humanism. Yet it built itself upon Petrarch's fabricated notion that philosophy is a hidden teaching. It simply rejected the historicist grounds for this teaching.

This is the context against which we have to understand the educational revolution of Rousseau and the Enlightenment. In his famous work Émile or On Education, Rousseau completes the trinity of the modern educational revolutions. Rousseau does this by reconstituting the Cartesian project by returning the notion philosophy to its historicist, Petrarchian and poetic origins.[15]

As part of the discovery of science completely whole in his mind as a system of clear and distinct ideas, Descartes could not account for communication between substances. He could not explain how mind and matter interact. Rousseau solved this problem by getting rid of the notion of matter and of Descartes's claim that, through application of simple Cartesian doubt, we find the system of science whole and complete in our minds. Rousseau turned matter into spirit and declared that, while science is a system of clear and distinct ideas, we discover it historically, not through Cartesian doubt. Instead, we find it through conflict with

---

[15] For a sustained defense of this claim, see Peter A. Redpath, *Masquerade of the Dream Walkers: Prophetic Theology from the Cartesians to Hegel* (Amsterdam and Atlanta: Editions Rodopi, B.V., 1998), 67–99.

Chapter 4: The Ideal of a University

poetic projections of our emotions, or what a contemporary *Heideggerian* would delight in calling our 'projects.'[16]

For our purposes, we need to understand that our contemporary Western educational institutions are the result of the application to the practical order of Enlightenment principles about the nature of philosophy and science. These Enlightenment principles gave birth to our modern public schools and universities. And the undergraduate and graduate education programs from these universities, plus the views of human nature popularized therein, and in disciplines of psychology, sociology, philosophy, biology, and others, have invaded our Catholic and non-Catholic educational institutions. They threaten their identity and health and the future well being of our democracy.

In short, mainly under the influence of Rousseau's and Descartes's disordered notions of science, the Enlightenment project unwittingly, and despite any and all claims to the contrary, gave birth to educational institutions that are essentially religious and sophistic forms of neo-pagan, neo-gnostic, spiritualistic fideism. These arose as the necessary means for engendering the poetic metaphysical ground of modern science.

The reason why this must be so is clear. Under the influence of Descartes , Rousseau, and their progeny, modern physical science seeks to be intellectually all-consuming, to replace metaphysics as

---

[16] Redpath, *Masquerade of the Dream Walkers: Prophetic Theology from the Cartesians to Hegel*, 67–99.

the highest form of human learning. No philosophical metaphysics can justify this pursuit. So, the modern scientific spirit turns to poetic myth, sophistry, and fideistic spirituality to create the metaphysics it needs to justify its all-consuming nature. In practical terms, this means that, if universities are primarily institutes of higher education, and metaphysics is the highest form of human education, the modern scientific spirit necessarily inclines us to create institutes of sophistry to justify its claim to be the highest mode of human knowing.

Most critics today correctly call these neo-gnostic religious principles 'secular humanism.' They wrongly call them a 'philosophy.' Educationally, under the influence of Rousseau, these principles maintain that all learning is revelation, a revelation of the something they call the 'human spirit.' By 'human spirit' they do not mean some sort of irrepressible emotion to greatness within the soul of every individual. They mean some sort of universal scientific spirit (the spirit of progress, of true human freedom, of the human project) that grows by first revealing itself in forms of backward Scriptural writings and organized religious practices. This is the same sort of universal, anti-Catholic, anti-Semitic spirit that was a main cause of the development of Fascism, Nazism, and Marxism.[17]

---

[17] For a sustained defense of these claims, see my "Anti-Semitism as an Enlightenment Metaphysical Principle," *Contemporary Philosophy*, 23: 3 & 4 (May/June & July/August 2001), 3–13.

Chapter 4: The Ideal of a University

To help us grow beyond these backward forms of religious understanding, Enlightened intellectuals think they must encourage students to question parental authority and must attack religious traditions as backward. They call this attack against authority 'tolerance' and 'questioning belief systems.' As a result, contemporary public schools have largely degenerated into neo-pagan religious institutes, schools of sophistry, re-education camps, to indoctrinate these Enlightened religious principles into students to foster the growth of true, progressive science from backward religion. Today, wittingly and unwittingly, many of our Catholic schools ape these institutions. We meet, today, to get out of this neo-gnostic mess and move the direction of education back to its proper pursuit: wisdom.

Toward the end of Plato's dialogue the *Gorgias*, Socrates tells the sophistic politician Callicles that a major difference exists between the lives of a philosopher and a sophist. The sophist denies the reality of good and evil, truth and falsity. For the sophist, man is the measure of all things and, at best, the human good is pleasure.

If such be the case, then no real art exists, and certainly no hierarchy of arts. To live the life of a sophist or a philosopher, Socrates tells us we need more than simply to exist. We must act. We must have power to pursue a life of pleasure or wisdom. To do this, the sophist must acquire the method of pursuing lifelong pleasure, the power to acquire undisturbed pleasure. He must, in short, become a panderer, a friend of despots.[18]

In my estimation, what Socrates tells us is true of individual sophists is also true of institutes of sophistry. Increasingly, since the Enlightenment, under the aim of engendering science as a system, and of creating a new political order based upon this sophistic dream, we in the West have created educational institutions suited to realize this project: institutes of sophistry that necessarily survive and flourish by pandering to corrupt politicians who help these institutes get the student loans, research dollars, and foreign students that they need to survive. This no is aberration of the Enlightenment. It is a metaphysical law: *agere sequitur esse*. Things tend to act according to their being.

Given this context, philosophically considered, what is the nature of a contemporary university, of a university that will help to extricate us from this mis-educational nightmare and restore learning to its proper order? Philosophically to answer this question involves philosophically to consider the problem. For the ancient Greeks, philosophy was not a logical system of ideas, and it never started as a study of abstract essences, not even for Plato.[19] *It was always born in the sensation of wonder.*

For the ancient Greeks, wonder was the first principle of philosophical investigation in general and in relation to all the

---

[18] Plato, *Gorgias*, 481B–522E.

[19] For a sustained defense of these claims, see *Redpath Wisdom's Odyssey*, 1–29.

divisions of philosophy. For the Greeks, philosophy always started as a natural act of wonder, rooted in a desire to escape from the potential damage that can accrue to us from being in a state of ignorance of being, the one, the true, the good, and the beautiful. All human beings by nature desire to know, as Aristotle tells us.[20]

By nature, we all desire to measure things, to beautify our surroundings, and most especially, to live well. These natural desires, coupled with the fear of the real damage that we recognize our ignorance can cause to our ability to satisfy these natural desires, generate in some of us the desire to escape from ignorance.

This subsequent desire originates in us in the same way that Plato tells us cities originate: through a recognition that we are not self-sufficient, that we are weak.[21] In my opinion, by natural desire, any genuine university originates in the same way that Plato tells us an ideal city originates, or Aristotle indicates that a state develops: through a social contract rooted in natural desire for mutual self-improvement made among people possessed of skill. Just as a city grows in a sort of widening circle from the unification of familial skills into community skills, and of community skills into skills needed to build villages, towns, cities, and states, so universities are extensions of home schooling, extensions of skills we first learn through participation in families.[22]

---

[20] Aristotle, *Metaphysics*, Bk. 1, ch. 1, 980a21–28.

[21] Plato, *Republic*, Bk. 2, 369B4–7.

[22] Plato, *Republic*, Bk. 4, 424A–426E and Aristotle, *Politics*, Bk. 1, ch. 1.

Historically, in the West, we see this process of growth in development of learning from the family into communities through the influence of ancient poets. Then, as villages, towns, and cities grew, professional schools of sophistry (rhetoric) and philosophy battled with poets for the development of higher education. As education became more universal, religious fraternities gave birth to cathedral and monastic schools, to houses of study, and eventually, in the twelfth century to the first university, Bologna.[23]

The lessons I learn from this development is that, in the West, universities arose from within widening political orders capable of supporting specific types of friendship among people possessed of specific learning skills, especially linguistic skills. The reason this occurred appears clear. Mortimer J. Adler has rightly advised us that we cannot become higher educated unless we read things that are over our heads.[24] By doing this, we often extend our intellectual ability because this exercise requires us to "stretch our imaginations." Before we can conceive anything, we must first be capable of imagining it. This means that a stretch of the human imagination always precedes theoretical, practical, and productive intellec-

---

[23] Gilson, *History of Christian Philosophy in the Middle Ages*, 246–250, McInerny, *A History of Western Philosophy*, 157–218, and Curtius, *European Literature and the Latin Middle Ages*, 17–57.

[24] Mortimer J. Adler, *How to Read a Book* (London: Jarrolds Publishers, Ltd., 1949).

tual advances on the levels of conceptualization, judgment, and reasoning.

We stretch the imagination, however, through analogy, through an interplay of our senses, intellect, memory, and anticipation, through what we might well call 'musings,' by comparing what is to what was and what could be. Such musings involve dreaming lofty, *but really possible*, dreams, of what could be, but is not and has not been. Unless we dream such dreams, we cannot form the images and imaginations that great discoverers and inventors need and use to make higher educational advances.

Adler tells us, too, that a great university is a university at which great teachers teach, teachers like Socrates, Plato, Archimedes, Aristotle, Sts. Augustine and Thomas, Dante Kepler, Galileo, and so on.[25] I concur. But a great university is also an association of great learners, with great methods of learning. At the start of his *Summa contra gentiles*, St. Thomas tells us that the office, *moral duty* (*officium*) of the wise man is "to set things in order and govern them well" and to do this about the most lofty matters: as far as possible to know the whole truth about everything that is (including religion) and refute opposing errors to this truth.[26] As the highest institution of human learning, clearly, a great, or ideal, university should have this same charge: to produce men and women of wisdom, who know as much as

---

[25] Adler, *How to Read a Book* 52–59.
[26] St. Thomas Aquinas, *Summa contra gentiles*, Bk. 1, ch. 1.

humanly possible about the whole truth accessible to the human person.

A university, however, has this specific charge as a university, not as a family, or a cathedral, school. Wisdom presupposes science. Science presupposes art. And art presupposes much experience. If the wise man or woman is a person with science who has mastered the loftiest reasoning habits to be had in a specific area of human learning, then human wisdom only comes to us after much specialization. And specialization only comes to us after much generalization.

Becoming wise is the work of a lifetime. Universities do not finish this life-long work. They continue students on the natural human pursuit of wisdom in a higher way: as independent learners. An ideal university, in short, ends the students need for learning by schooling. Hence, when a student graduates from such an institution, further learning by schooling should be a choice, not a necessity.

This means that university education presupposes college education, and college education presupposes much undergraduate education. Primarily, universities are graduate schools, intellectual associations that aim at specialization in areas of theoretical, practical, and productive science. At a university, through conversation with great intellects, through reading their books, we should learn to discover the first and most universal principles at work in the arts and sciences.

To be able to do this we need the requisite imaginative, conceptual, judgmental, and reasoning skills to stretch our imaginations and intellects beyond the skills of a generalist. If we want to think like a mathematical, chemical, or musical specialist, we must first be able to imagine the way these people do. And we cannot learn to imagine like a specialist until, on the college and pre-college levels, we have first learned how to become good general listeners and readers. Higher education, in short, grows as a widening circle grows.

All along the way, from its first beginnings until its deepest mastery, human learning involves an ever-widening and deepening interplay among poetry, in the sense of good literature, rhetoric, logic, and other forms of learning. On the highest level this interplay involves philosophy and theology.

To reach this level with maximum intensity we have to make sure to avoid confounding philosophy with one or more of the liberal arts. The liberal arts prepare a student's external and internal sense faculties, reason and appetites for higher learning by beautifying the soul, no by inculcating highly abstract theoretical truths. The aim of an art is real goodness or beauty, not abstract theoretical truth.

Beauty and goodness are real qualities, perfections, as real as defects. Today, we speak about with reality of defects, of defective quality of material, with ease, but tend to shy away from referring to materials as having perfections. This makes no sense. Things cannot be defective unless they can be perfective.

Beauty and goodness are qualities that perfect things. Hence, we tend to identify artists, people with skill, with people possessed of an ability to remove defects from material and impart qualities that improve a material. For example, a manufacturer who produces a beautiful quality tape recording or CD makes a material object that can convey a sound pleasing to the ear with a high quantity of intensity, a sound so pleasing that it: (1) overwhelms the matter with the completeness of its goodness and, in the process; and (2) shocks the human senses, appetites, and intellect through the magnitude of its natural suitability for the faculties involved.

Liberal artists do a similar thing. Through their arts they remove from human faculties defects that prevent these faculties from exercising their natural acts of knowing with a high quantity of intensity. And they impart in their place beautifying qualities, habits of mind, memory, imagination, and external sense of high intensity that improve the precise exercise of these faculties in performance of their natural acts under direction of a healthy reasoning faculty.

Put in scholastic terms, higher education involves increasing habituation of the agent intellect whereby we become increasingly capable of precisely judging about different kinds of things through universal concepts that we are increasingly capable of abstracting from sense images. These acts of abstraction are the work of philosophy, not of poetry, rhetoric, or logic. As St. Thomas said centuries ago, "The seven liberal arts do not sufficiently divide theoretical philosophy" ("*Septem artes liberales non sufficienter dividunt philosophiam*"). Nonetheless, analogous stretching of the human imagination through qualities of poetry, rhetoric, and logic, are indispensable handmaidens, necessary, but not sufficient, conditions, to developing the philosophical intellect's increase in its ability to engage in these different kinds of intellectual abstraction.[27]

An ideal university, in short, must be a house of studies and wisdom, a fraternal association of scholars that rightly orders the relationship among the arts and sciences so that, like Plato's just man, each can do its own business, through its own principles, while each contributes to the development of a well-ordered person. No such institution can do this job well where the different arts and sciences do not recognize and respect what each does for the good of the whole, where the practitioners of arts and sciences do not know their respective subjects, principles, and methods, and where intellectual goals are subordinated to political agendas.

If we wish to reverse the downward spiral of higher education in the West, and create a real renaissance in education, then our crucial agenda must be this: to be right about the nature of the

---

[27] St. Thomas Aquinas, *Commentary on the De Trinitate of Boethius, Questions V and VI. St. Thomas Aquinas: The Division and Methods of the Sciences*, trans. with an introduction and notes, Armand A. Maurer (Toronto: Pontifical Institute of Mediaeval Studies, 1963), q. 5, a. 1, ad 3, p. 11. See, also, Curtius, *European Literature and the Latin Middle Ages*, 57.

thing we seek to bring into being and to reason prudently about its generation. If we do these things, politics will take care of itself. As Plato realized, rightly ordered institutions of higher learning will help to develop good citizens, and good citizens will help to develop good politicians and good cities. Our job at present is firmly to fix our sight on the goal at hand and, with God's help, to set things in order and govern them well. The task that lies before us is enormous, but doable. Whatever its magnitude, we have little choice but to forge ahead. If we do not do this, who else will, or can?

Chapter 5

Petrarch's Failed Project

Etienne Gilson's classic book, *The Unity of Philosophical Experience*, is a historical-philosophical thriller about what hap-pens to philosophical teachings once they leave the abstract thought of philosophers and these thinkers and their students, or disciples, try to put them into practice in the real world. Gilson tells this tale by weaving together two principles, which he takes from history and philosophy, especially from metaphysics.[1]

While Gilson does not say so explicitly, from metaphysics, he takes the classical scholastic principle that we tend to act according to our natures. Hence, a dog will tend to act like a dog, a cat like a cat, and so on. He extends and transposes this principle to human behavior and comes up with a more specific principle regarding human psychology: We human beings think the way we can, not the way we wish.[2]

---

[1] Étienne Gilson, *The Unity of Philosophical Experience* (New York: Charles Scribner's Sons [1937], 1965). This article is a revised version of a two-part talk I gave on 10 April 2002 at the Catholic University of Lublin [KUL] entitled, "Petrarch's Dream and the Modern Project: A Chapter Gilson did not Write," published in Poland under the title "*Marzenie Petrarki I nowoczesny projekt: rozdzxiat, którego Gilson nie napisat*," trans. Pawel Tarasiewicz, *Czlowiek w kulturze* [*Man in Culture*] (Lublin: Fundacja Lubelska Szkola Filozofii Chrzescijanskiej [Lublin

From this extension and transposition, Gilson makes a further extension and transposition to history, and derives the historical principle that, once we accept a specific philosophical teaching, and then attempt to apply it to reality that teaching takes on a life of its own, leading, perhaps, to consequences that its author never envisioned and with which its author might vehemently disagree.

From history alone, Gilson makes the observation that, often, philosophers tend not to learn from philosophical experience. Once we find that our principles do not work when we try to apply them with logical consistency to the real world, instead of rejecting our principles, we often try to dodge the consequences of our foolishness by rejecting the ways of the world, not the ways of our false principles.[3]

In another classic tale, *Reason and Revelation in the Middle Ages*, which Gilson wrote subsequent to *The Unity of Philosophical Experience*, he makes a startling statement. He tells any historian who might investigate the sources of "modern rationalism" (the tendency to exaggerate scientific reason to make it the only explanation for everything) that an uninterrupted chain of influence exists from the Averroistic tradition of the Master of Arts of Paris to

---

School of Christian Philosophy], 15 (2003). I thank the editor Piotr Jaeszhński permission to publish in here in its revised form.

[2] Gilson, *The Unity of Philosophical Experience*, 301–302.

[3] Gilson, *The Unity of Philosophical Experience*, 299–320.

Chapter 5: Petrarch's Failed Project 119

the European freethinkers of the seventeenth and eighteenth centuries (the so-called 'Age of Reason'.[4]

This statement is startling for at least two reasons: (1) Despite the extensive influence that Gilson observes of the Averroistic tradition from the Master of Arts of Paris to the modern and Enlightenment freethinkers, nowhere in *The Unity of Philosophical Experience*, or in any other work that I know of, does Gilson go into the fine details of the historical and philosophical evolution of this tradition from the Renaissance to the seventeenth and eighteenth centuries. (2) Had Gilson done so, by applying the same principles he had used in *The Unity of Philosophical Experience*, he would have verified more extensively the philosophical and historical principles he had used in that work. And, simultaneously, he would have had to reject some major conclusions he had drawn about the development of modern thought, especially a claim he made about René Descartes: that Descartes marks the transition from the scepticism of Montaigne to the modern period of constructive thinking in philosophy.

As I have indicated in my book *Cartesian Nightmare: An Introduction to Transcendental Sophistry*, in making this assertion,

---

[4] Étienne Gilson, *Reason and Revelation in the Middle Ages* (New York: Charles Scribner's Sons, 1938), 65. I thank James V. Schall, S.J. (r.i.p.). for recalling this passage to my attention. See his article, "Possessed of Both a Reason and a Revelation," *A Thomistic Tapestry: Essays in Memory of Étienne Gilson* ed. Peter A. Redpath (Amsterdam and Atlanta: Editions Rodopi, B. V., 2002).

Gilson was wrong about Descartes on two counts: (1) Descartes is much more than a transition from Montaigne's skepticism to the modern period and (2) Descartes could not have moved reasoning from skepticism to "constructive thinking in philosophy" for the simple reason that, strictly speaking, Descartes was no philosopher and, if anything, his influence on modernity was anti-philosophical and philosophically deconstructive, not philosophical and philosophically constructive.[5]

Descartes did not move the West from the skepticism of Montaigne to a new philosophy. He moved the West from the predominance of one branch of the classical liberal arts, the *trivium* (the poetry and rhetoric of Renaissance humanism) to another, the *quadrivium*.[6] Strictly speaking, Descartes did not generate a new philosophy or a return to constructive philosophical thinking. He wedded together a new rhetoric and poetic view of the world in which mathematical abstraction united to a new logic of invention, not the rhetoric and poetic view of the world that had dominated Renaissance humanism, would prevail as the primary means by which Westerners would, from that point on, read the Book of Nature.[7]

---

[5] Peter A. Redpath, *Cartesian Nightmare: An Introduction to Transcendental Sophistry* (Amsterdam and Atlanta: Editions Rodopi, B. V., 1997), 20. See Gilson, *The Unity of Philosophical Experience*, 125–126.

[6] The classical *trivium* consisted of the arts of grammar, rhetoric, and logic. The *quadrivium* consisted of arithmetic, geometry, astronomy, and music.

[7] Redpath, *Cartesian Nightmare*, 20.

Chapter 5: Petrarch's Failed Project

In so doing, the dream of Descartes became heir to the legacy of an earlier dream and political project, of Francesco Petrarcha (Petrarch): to revive Roman culture by reviving classical poetry and rhetoric.[8] In so doing, I maintain that Descartes became the main modern link for the uninterrupted chain of the Averroistic tradition from the Master of Arts of Paris to seventeenth- and eighteenth-century freethinkers. In this paper, I give the general outlines of how this transmission occurred and the role that Petrarch and Descartes played in it.

To do so, I need to return for a moment to one day in Rome in 1341 when Petrarch was crowned poet laureate. Renowned Renaissance historian Paul Oskar Kristeller says that, on this day: (1) "The reading of the ancient Latin writers, and the sight of Rome's ancient monuments, evoked in Petrarch as in many other Italian humanists a strong nostalgia for the political greatness of the Roman Republic and Empire"; (2) "the hope to restore this greatness was the central political idea that guided" Petrarch in his dealings with the Pope and Emperor, with Cola di Rienzo, and with the various Italian governments"; and (3) the conviction that his coronation was a renewal in his person of "an ancient Roman honor."[9]

---

[8] Peter A. Redpath, *Wisdom's Odyssey from Philosophy to Transcendental Sophistry* (Amsterdam and Atlanta: Editions Rodopi, B. V., 1997), 86; Redpath, *Cartesian Nightmare*, 53; Paul Oskar Kristeller, *Eight Philosophers of the Italian Renaissance* (Stanford: Stanford University Press, 1966), 7.

[9] Kristeller, *Eight Philosophers of the Italian Renaissance* (Stanford: Stanford University Press, 1966), 7.

The significance of this event is crucial to understand. Historians of Renaissance thought generally credit Petrarch with being the single-most important influence on the development of Renaissance humanism. Charles Trinkhaus has called him, "The most potently formative individual in the evolution of the humanist movement."[10] In this respect, we may call him, if not the Father of Renaissance humanism, the "Father of the Renaissance project."

Fully to appreciate the significance of this project and its influence on the direction of subsequent Western thought, we need to recall that Renaissance humanism was a rhetorical and poetic, not a philosophical, movement. As Kristeller repeatedly tells us, the Renaissance humanists were not primarily philosophers. They were rhetoricians and poets, heirs to schools of the liberal arts at places like Paris and Oxford, who brought their modes of thinking to Renaissance Italy by emigrating there from France and England. Petrarch used this movement for a political project: to revive the greatness of Roman culture. More specifically, Petrarch's dream was to revive Roman culture through a study of the classics, of the pagan poets and rhetoricians, especially of people like Vergil and

---

[10] Charles Trinkhaus, *In Our Image and Likeness: Humanity and Divinity in Italian Humanist Thought*, 2 vols. (Chicago: University of Chicago Press, 1970), vol. 2, 684. See, also, Redpath, *Wisdom's Odyssey*, 86–98.

Chapter 5: Petrarch's Failed Project

Cicero.[11] In a nutshell, this was what Italian Renaissance humanism was all about.

In so doing, Petrarch had a problem. To revive Roman culture Petrarch had to revive an interest in the classical poetry and rhetoric of Greece and Rome. The classical poets and rhetoricians, however, were pagans.[12] And the poets were polytheists and complete materialists. Among other things, in fourteenth-century standards, they rejected the by-then well-established Western theological principles of God's unity and immateriality. They also told fantastic stories about the gods, portraying them, at times, as wife- and child-beaters, adulterers, rapists, even cannibals. Their depiction of the gods was so fantastic that Socrates rejected it, and speculated that, perhaps, his rejection of this incredible, poetic view of the gods was part of the reason he had made so many enemies in Athens.[13]

For such reasons, for centuries, the Roman Catholic Church had not encouraged reading of pagan poets. In the Medieval *trivium* poetry was not even a separate division. The division was

---

[11] Paul Oskar Kristeller, *Renaissance Thought: The Classic, Scholastic, and Humanist Strains* (New York: Harper & Row, Publishers, 1961), 109. See, also, Charles Trinkhaus, *In Our Image and Likeness: Humanity and Divinity in Italian Humanist Thought*, 2 vols. (Chicago: University of Chicago Press, 1970), vol. 1, 23; and Redpath, *Wisdom's Odyssey*, 72–73, 92–97.

[12] Redpath, *Wisdom's Odyssey*, 1–29.

[13] Plato, *Euthyphro* 5D–6C.

grammar, rhetoric, and logic. Because of extensive illiteracy during the Carolingian Renaissance, grammar and rhetoric played a more important role in the schools than did poetry. Poetry was then taught within the liberal arts division of rhetoric as part of the art of letter writing (*ars dictaminis*). Still, it was largely the Cinderella of the liberal arts.[14]

Petrarch had another problem, involving academic disputes going back for centuries, to Plato's time and beyond. During this Middle Ages these disputes had resurfaced between theologians and members of the faculty of arts in the monastic and cathedral schools, and, later, among members of the faculty of arts at the University of Paris: the famed 'Battle of the Arts.'[15] While many contemporary thinkers do not realize it, this fight was simply a continuation of the age-old battle among philosophers and poets that Plato described in Book 10 of his famous *Republic*.[16] This brawl would continue into the thirteenth century in Paris, where Henry of Andelys would describe it in his *Battle of the Seven Liberal Arts*, and Petrarch would redirect it during the fourteenth century.[17]

---

[14] Redpath *Wisdom's Odtssey*, 50–56, 72–73, 93; Kristeller, *Eight Philosophers of the Italian Renaissance*, 150; Trinkhaus, *In Our Image and Likeness*, vol. 2, 685., *Wisdom's Odyssey*, 1–29.

[15] Redpath, *Wisdom's Odtssey*, 63–86.

[16] Plato, *Republic*, Bk. 10, 595A–607B.

[17] Redpath, *Wisdom's Odtssey*, 68. See, also, Étienne Gilson, *History of Christian Philosophy in the Middle Ages* (New York: Random House, 7th printing, 1955).

During the twelfth century, the West did not have a unified view of philosophy. The major intellectual institutions at the time were the monastic school of St. Victor in Paris and cathedral school of Chartres. At these centers, a Ciceronian notion of philosophy as a discipline which investigates "all things human and divine" co-existed with a notion that philosophy was identical with the traditional liberal arts, notably the *trivium*.[18] As we might expect, these different views of philosophy eventually overflowed into squabbles about which liberal art was higher in the curriculum than another, which, in turn, overflowed into fights with theologians. "For example, at Chartres, in the twelfth century, William of Conches and John of Salisbury, and Hugh of St. Victor became embroiled in a battle between dialecticians and anti-dialecticians [that is, logicians and anti-logicians], involving charges and counter-charges of heresy and watering down the school curriculum (the Cornifician controversy), which eventually caused William to abandon his teaching at Chartres."[19]

Actually, the Ciceronian notion of philosophy and the identification of philosophy with the liberal arts were equally wrong. St.

---

[18] Redpath, *Wisdom's Odyssey*, 68; Ralph M. McInerny, *A History of Western Philosophy.Philosophy from St. Augustine to Ockham* (Notre Dame, Ind. and London: University of Notre Dame Press, 1970), 89–202; Gilson, *History of Christian Philosophy in the Middle Ages*, 140–178.

[19] Redpath, *Wisdom's Odyssey*, 68; Ralph M. McInerny, *A History of Western Philosophy.Philosophy from St. Augustine to Ockham*, 89–202; Gilson, *History of Christian Philosophy in the Middle Ages*, 140–178.All materials in brackets and parenthesis in all footnotes are my addition.

Thomas Aquinas had rightly recognized that, for the ancient Greeks, philosophy was not the liberal arts. And it was not the study of all things human and divine. The Middle Ages inherited these mistaken notions of philosophy from Church Fathers, rhetoricians such as St. Augustine, and enclopedists like Cassiodorus and Isiodore of Seville, who had passed them on to thinkers in Medieval cathedral and monastic schools.[20] Despite Aquinas, eventually, thinkers in these schools would pass these erroneous notions on to Petrarch. And, through Descartes, Petrarch and his progeny would pass them on to us.[21]

Petrarch's more specific role as (1) a character in this story of historical transmission of mistakes about the nature of philosophy and real-life consequences, and (2) his role as a chapter in Gilson's story, arises from his political project and the means he sought to effect it.

Precisely, the tale unfolds thus. Petrarch wanted to revive the greatness of Roman culture. To do this he needed to revive an interest in reading pagan writers, especially rhetoricians and poets. To do this, he needed, in turn, to elevate the status of poets and rhetoricians in the university and within the eyes of the Church. To elevate this status, he took a commonly traveled road in the history of human thought: He sought to increase the status of the

---

[20] Redpath, *Wisdom's Odyssey*, 43, 189–202; Trinkhaus, *In Our Image and Likeness*, vol. 2, 695.

[21] For a detailed study of Descartes as continuing the tradition of Renaissance poetry and rhetoric, see Redpath, *Cartesian Nightmare*.

disciplines of poetry and rhetoric within the order of human learning and the eyes of Church authorities by decreasing the status and misinterpreting the nature of other academic disciplines, especially, some versions of scholastic theology.[22]

Paradoxically, wittingly or unwittingly, the road Petrarch took had already been traveled by one of his arch-enemies: Averroes. During the twelfth century, in a book entitled *On the Harmony of Religion and Philosophy*, Averroes had sophistically reworked Plato's view of learning [symbolized by Plato through a divided line] in an attempt to safeguard the rights and freedom of philosophy against intrusion by theologians and others.[23]

This reconstruction consisted of distinguishing three categories of human minds and three corresponding degrees and limits of human understanding, learning, and teaching "of one single and same truth": (1) the most true and abstract scientific mind of the philosopher, which supposedly apprehends, learns, and teaches this truth in an absolute sense in its hidden, interior meaning, through demonstrative reasoning "from the necessary to the necessary by the necessary"; (2) the less true and symbolic unscientific mind of the logician, and theologian, which grasps this truth in its exterior, imaginative, symbolic meaning, through logical interpretation and probability; and (3) the simple religious

---

[22] Redpath, *Wisdom's Odyssey*, 86–98.
[23] Averroes, *On the Harmony of Religion and Philosophy*, trans. George F. Hourani (London: Luzac, 1961). See, also, Plato, *Republic*, Bk. 6, 509D–511E.

and believing mind, which apprehends this one and same truth through the imagination, emotions, and oratorical arguments.[24]

Gilson adds that, while "the Koran is truth itself," Averroes maintained that the Koran "has an exterior and symbolic meaning for the uninstructed, an interior and hidden meaning for scholars." And he considered revelation's true meaning to be its most lofty meaning. Its most lofty meaning, however, was its philosophical, or scientific, meaning. Averroes thought that philosophical truth is "the highest type of human truth." This means that, for Averroes: (1) human truth is the highest type of Koranic truth, (2) the highest type of human truth is philosophy, or science, (3) philosophical, or scientific, truth is present in a hidden fashion in the Koran, and (4) only philosophers can recognize it!

Gilson acutely observes that two consequences immediately result from Averroes's threefold division of the human mind: (1) "a mind should never seek to raise itself above the degree of interpretation of which it is capable"; and (2) "one should never divulge to inferior classes of minds the interpretations reserved for the superior classes." Averroes thought that philosophers had made the precise mistake of "untimely communication of superior knowledge to inferior minds." The immediate consequence was

---

[24] Gilson, *History of Christian Philosophy in the Middle Ages*, 218–219.

Chapter 5: Petrarch's Failed Project 129

the rise of "hybrid methods" of interpretation that: (1) "mix oratorical art, dialectics, and demonstration" and (2) "are the inexhaustible source of heresies."[25]

Unhappily for subsequent philosophical history, Petrarch took and adapted Averroes's division of human minds by designing (1) his own program and method for harmonizing religion and philosophy and (2) a new, fabricated interpretation of philosophy's history to support it.

In Petrarch's program a new mind and profession replaced the trinitarian hierarchy of Averroes. In Petrarch's scheme, the highest form of human mind is that of the theologizing poet *poetae theologisantes* [theologizing poets], not the mind of the philosopher. As a complement of this new mind in the order of teaching and learning, Petrarch created a new profession of poetry that combines the techniques of rhetoric, poetry, and theology: *theologia poetica* [poetic theology].

In this Petrachian intellectual program, true philosophy, religion, and rhetoric become identical. To support this program, among other things, Petrarch cited: (1) the authority of history, including testimony of Scripture, leading philosophers, Aristotle,

---

[25] Gilson, *History of Christian Philosophy in the Middle Ages*, 218–219.

Isiodore of Seville, saintly authority, St. Augustine, and (2) the name "poet."[26]

As part of this support, Petrarch falsely maintained that the ancient poets (1) were not polytheists and (2) did not literally accept the depiction of the gods that they gave to the "vulgar" or mass of mankind. He maintained that the ancient poets were closet monotheists and did not accept the gods to be adulterers and deceivers. He believed "that only a madman would worship adulterers and liars as gods."[27]

Petrarch supported his contention by considering the origin of poetry and citing the *Etymologies* of the early Medieval Christian encyclopedist Isiodore of Seville. According to Petrarch, in that work, Isiodore: "recounts how ancient poetry arose among 'rude men' who were first discovering a desire to know the divine and who realized that such a superhuman power deserved to be revered in a super-human ceremony and an awe-inspiring ritual. To accomplish this ceremony and ritual, these men built elaborate temples, made vessels of gold and purple robes, and established a priesthood."[28]

---

[26] Redpath, *Wisdom's Odyssey*, 93; Trinkhaus, *In Our Image and Likeness*, vol. 2, 683–721; Kristeller, *Eight Philosophers of the Italian Renaissance*, 17, 150–155.

[27] Redpath, *Wisdom's Odyssey*, 97–98; Trinkhaus, *In Our Image and Likeness*, vol. 2, 689–698.

[28] Redpath, *Wisdom's Odyssey*, 97–98; Trinkhaus, *In Our Image and Likeness*, vol. 2, 689–698.

Petrarch observed that, thus constructed, ancient "ritual was silent." To make it talk in an appropriate way, Petrarch maintained that the ancient poets fashioned:

> a method of speaking proportionate to the magnitude of the praise they wished to convey. Because they wanted to please the divinity, they fashioned an elegant style of speaking, one in no way vulgar or plebian, out of the high-sounding words and interesting and charming metres. They could not create an exquisite language in a vulgar form. To do so is impossible. They had to use a lofty art. In Greek, this art was called "poetic." Hence, . . . those who practiced this are were called "poets."[29]

Petrarch thought that all this evidence showed beyond reasonable doubt that the ancient poets (*prisci poetae*) were: (1) ancient theologians [*prisci theologi*], (2) recognized as such by the ancient Greeks, and (3) 'closet monotheists and culture critics.'[30]

Considered as such, he contended that Christians should not consider reading ancient poets a threat to Christianity. While the 'vulgar' might not understand their words' hidden meaning, Pet-

---

[29] Redpath, *Wisdom's Odyssey*, 97–98; Trinkhaus, *In Our Image and Likeness*, vol. 2, 689–698.

[30] Redpath, *Wisdom's Odyssey*, 97–98; Trinkhaus, *In Our Image and Likeness*, vol. 2, 689–698.

rarch maintained that any "intelligent Christians can easily recognize the obvious absurdities and illusory nature of mythology. If we look deep enough into their hidden meaning, we will eventually find the true philosophy of universal Christian revelation, the Word Made Flesh, the only real, living universal working occultly in nature."[31]

In short, to elevate the status of poetry within Western higher education and culture, Petrarch fabricated an anagogical tale, a prophetic theology, about the nature and origin of philosophy. In this fiction, (1) Christian revelation became identified with an esoteric teaching called 'true philosophy' and (2) poetry and the works of the ancient poets became the prophetic vehicle through which this true philosophy was protected and transmitted to intellectual elites across generations.

Knowingly or not, in creating this fictional account about the nature and origin of philosophy, in his own way and making the appropriate changes, Petrarch repeated the mental division of Averroes and revived an apocryphal story about the origins of philosophy that had apparently first arisen, as an apologetic defense, with Alexandrian Jews in Antiquity.

Centuries before Petrarch and Averroes, using apologetic reasons similar to Petrarch's, Jews living in Alexandria had fabricated a false history about the nature and origin of philosophy. To de-

---

[31] Redpath, *Wisdom's Odyssey*, 97–98; Trinkhaus, *In Our Image and Likeness*, vol. 2, 689–698.

fend themselves against attacks by ancient pagan Greeks and Romans that they were cultureless barbarians, these Jewish thinkers had claimed that philosophy was a hidden teaching first developed by Moses and stolen from the Jewish people and falsified by the Egyptians, Babylonians, Greeks, and so on. If these Jewish thinkers were right, Averroes had it all wrong. Moses, not Aristotle, was The Philosopher (*falsafah*).[32]

St. Ambrose had transmitted a version of this fabricated history to St. Aurelius Augustine. In his highly influential work *On Christian Doctrine* (*De doctrina christiana*), Augustine transmits it to the later Middle Ages. He tells his readers:

> whatever semblance of truth is in pagan philosophy . . . it is right and proper for Christians to appropriate for their own use. In so doing, Augustine, like Ambrose, thinks Christians, as heirs to the Israelites, are only taking back, from unjust possessors, what is rightfully theirs. He thinks that Plato probably learned about Jewish revelation when he had travelled to Egypt and that whatever the Platonists

---

[32] Redpath, *Wisdom's Odyssey*, 42–44; Redpath, *Cartesian Nightmare*, 7–9; Ernst Robert Curtius, *European Literature and the Latin Middle Ages*, trans. William R. Trask (New York: Published for the Bollingen Foundation by Pantheon Books, 1952), 39, 209–212.

say which is "good and truthful" they took from the Israelites.³³

As Aristotle warns us in his *On the Heavens* (*De caelo*) and Aquinas repeats at the beginning of his little treatise *On Being and Essence* (*De ente et essential*), small mistakes in the beginning of scientific research about 'first principles' eventually grow "to vast proportions."³⁴ Petrarch did not realize this when he laid down his false history of the nature and origin of philosophy as a supporting principle of his program for reviving Roman culture. He was short on philosophical experience, and prudence, common sense. Hence, his program was doomed eventually to fail. In the interim, other Renaissance humanists would come to his aid to embellish his story.

Giovanni Boccaccio would write *On the Genealogy of the Gods* (*De genealogia deorum*) in which he would trace the decline of true philosophy, and with it monotheism, from its origin with Moses through its corruption at the hands of Noah's descendants, and

---

³³ Redpath, *Wisdom's Odyssey*, 47; St. Aurelius Augustine, *On Christian Doctrine*, trans. D. W. Robertson, Jr. (Indianapolis and New York: The Bobbs-Merrill Company, Inc. 1958), 64, 75.

³⁴ St. Thomas Aquinas, *On Being and Essence*, trans. with an introduction and notes, 2d rev. ed. (Toronto: Pontifical Institute of Mediaeval Studies [1949], 1968), "Prologue," 29; Aristotle, *De caelo*, Bk. 1, ch. 5, 271b8–14.

revival by ancient poets. Eventually, he would show how the Plato contained the whole of Judaism and Homer![35]

Chapter 1 of Book 2 of Coluccio Salutati's *Four Books on the Labors of Hercules* (*Quatri libri de laboribus Herculis*) would add to Boccacio's tale by precisely locating the origin of the practice of idolatry through Chapter 14 of the *Book of Wisdom*, which traced the practice's provenance to a mourning father who had "fashioned an image of his dead son and required his slaves to worship it."[36]

Cristoforo Landino would, in turn, further specify the transmission of philosophy from Moses to Plato through Egyptian priests. And he would explain how Vergil became a student of Plato and, thereby, became the greatest poet and philosopher of antiquity.[37] Other thinkers, like Lorenzo Valla, Giannozzo Manetti, and Marsilio Ficino would further cement the Renaissance humanist identification of poetry, philosophy, and theology, using, among other devices, the Medieval allegory that nature is a book. Since nature is a holy book, and since only those capable of reading can apprehend the truths that lie hidden within a book, reading teachers (theological poets, rhetoricians, and grammarians) become the main vehicle through which book of nature enters the human mind.[38]

---

[35] Redpath, *Wisdom's Odyssey*, 98.
[36] Redpath, *Wisdom's Odyssey*, 98–99.
[37] Redpath, *Wisdom's Odyssey*, 102.
[38] Redpath, *Wisdom's Odyssey*, 95–125.

Abstractly considered, were it not for the metaphysical truth that things tend to act according to their natures, the Petrarchian dream appears unassailable. When he started his project, Petrarch never dreamed of the day when a mathematician named Galileo Galilei would write in *The Assayer*: "Philosophy is written in the greatest of books which stands always open to our gaze; I mean the universe; but it cannot be understood unless one first learns the language and the characters in which it is written. It is written in the language of mathematics and the characters are triangles, circles and other geometrical figures. . . . Without these . . . the investigation of nature is wandering in an obscure labyrinth."[39]

But when Galileo penned these short sentences, the Renaissance humanist age, where poetic imagination was bridled by theology and poets made their living mainly through service to the Church, had come to end. Petrarch had violated the first law to be inferred from philosophical experience: *"Philosophy always buries its undertakers."*[40] The yoke of the poets had now passed from Pope Julius to modern investment bankers, mathematicians, and physical scientists. In trying to bury philosophy through a faulty understanding of its nature, Petrarch had buried his own project. Poetry again became the Cinderella of the liberal arts!

---

[39] Redpath, *Wisdom's Odyssey*, 89, in A. Robert Caponigri, *A History of Western Philosophy*, Vol. 3, *Philosophy from the Renaissance to the Romantic Age* (University of Notre Dame Press: Notre Dame, Ind. and London, United Kingdom), 22.

[40] Gilson, *The Unity of Philosophical Experience*, 306.

Chapter 5: Petrarch's Failed Project

The battle of the arts previously fought by Averroes and Petrarch had now entered a new age, to become bridled and redirected by the dreams of a new poet laureate, the man now considered to be the modern *falsafah*, modern philosophy's 'Father,' René Descartes. In one of his major works, *Meditations on First Philosophy*, as Descartes would sit nostalgically surveying the ruins of the numerous false opinions in his soul, he would long to "raze everything to the ground," "begin again from the original foundations." With a new false method, and a new poetic garland to obscure and crown his understanding of the natures of things as modernity's new poet laureate, he would take the baton handed from Averroes to Petrarch and try to uncover the wondrous, 'true system of philosophy'—hidden, this time, in the recesses of his mind. After centuries of intellectual darkness, The 'Age of Reason' had finally begun.

Like Petrarch centuries before him, on this day, as *Poet Laureat of the Age of Reason, meditation on his own mind and the sight of it in ruins evoked in Descartes*: (1) a strong nostalgia to uncover the greatness of the wondrous system of science buried therein; (2) the hope to unleash this greatness became the central idea that guided him in his dealings thereafter; and (3) the conviction that his coronation was the beginning in his person of a new honor: the start of true philosophy as a system of clear and distinct ideas.[41]

---

[41] Redpath, *Cartesian Nightmare*, 53; René Descartes, *Meditations on First Philosophy*, in *René Descartes: Discourse on Method and Medita-*

Unhappily, like Petrarch, Descartes's project would eventually become buried by the operation of its own erroneous principles in human history.

During the sixteenth-century an Italian humanist named Polydore Vergilio had published a highly influential reference book entitled *De inventoribus rerum* [*On the Invention of Things*]. In this work, in a fashion similar to Petrarch, Boccaccio, and other Renaissance humanists, Vergilio had traced the origin of philosophy to Moses, from whom the Ionian Thales and the Italian Pythaogras purportedly initiated two new beginnings of philosophy, with the Italian Pythagoras coining the name 'philosophy.'

Regarding this purported new beginning of philosophy in antiquity in Italy, in his classic *History of Christian Philosophy in the Middle Ages,* Étienne Gilson summarily dismisses such a claim in one terse sentence: "Ancient Rome had produced no philosophy."[42] Gilson immediately adds that the Ciceronian tradition lasted throughout the Middle Ages and played a crucial role in the history of Western civilization. He maintains that, through Petrarch, this tradition "became a decisive factor in bringing about the revival of classical humanism." "[B]ut," he says, "one does not see any philosophical doctrine whose origin could be traced back

---

tions on First Philosophy, ed. and trans. Donald A. Cress, 3d edit. (Indianapolis, Ind. and Cambridge, Mass.: Hackett Publishing Company, Inc., 1993), 9–61.

[42] Étienne Gilson, *History of Christian Philosophy in the Middle Ages* (New York: Random House, 7th printing, 1955), 540.

Chapter 5: Petrarch's Failed Project

to any Roman writer. Cicero, Seneca, even Lucretius have been busy popularizing ideas of Greek origin; they did not add anything important to their sources. The philosophical sterility of ancient Rome seems to be a fact."[43]

Despite this fact, at the dawn of the modern age, Vergilio's *De inventoribus rerum* helped to popularize in the West the apocryphal notion of the nature and origin of philosophy that Petrarch and his Italian humanist followers had revived. While Petrarch's notion of the origin of philosophy appears to have been absent from Averroes, his idea of philosophy's general nature as a hidden teaching or system was substantially the same. In this way, the Averroistic idea of philosophy became a driving force underlying Renaissance humanism, which Vergilio would help pass on to Descartes and his contemporaries.

"Thanks, in part, to the recent invention of the Gutenberg press, Vergilio's work had appeared the thirty Latin editions by the time of the author's death in 1555," was "still influential in Leibniz's time," ". . . and by the early eighteenth century more than a hundred versions had accumulated in eight languages, including Russian."[44]

---

[43] Gilson, *History of Christian Philosophy in the Middle Ages*, 541.

[44] Redpath, *Cartesian Nightmare: An Introduction to Transcendental Sophistry*, 7–9. See, also, Brian P. Copenhaver and Charles B. Schmitt, *Renaissance Philosophy* (Oxford and New York: Oxford University Press, 1992), 329–337.

The first authors of modern histories of philosophy, like Thomas Stanley and Georg Horn, also helped to transmit this erroneous idea of the nature and origin of philosophy to modernity. These authors were humanist rhetoricians, not philosophers. Modern history, we should recall, was one of the disciplines developed by Renaissance rhetoricians. These humanist rhetoricians continued and solidified Vergilio's historical scholarship and "notion that philosophy is revealed, unitary system or body of truth which had been first given directly by God to Moses. They also popularized the claim that this hidden system of knowledge had been later buried in hermetic and cabalist writings, and had eventually been passed on through ancient pagan poets up to Plato and beyond."[45]

For my present purposes the import of this fabricated history of philosophy's nature and origin is that this was the prevailing view of philosophy when René Descartes came on the scene. Descartes enters our story at the tail end of the Renaissance, when this erroneous view of philosophy was in vogue and a new chapter was beginning in the battle of the arts.

This new chapter in the battle had something radically different about it. As a result, it has escaped the notice of many Western intellectuals, including, to some extent, Gilson. Previous battles of the arts, going back to Socrates, had generally occurred within the

---

[45] Redpath, *Cartesian Nightmare: An Introduction to Transcendental Sophistry*, 9. See, also, Copenhave and Schmitt, *Renaissance Philosophy*, 331–332.

Chapter 5: Petrarch's Failed Project

trivium, or between the *trivium* and philosophy and theology. This new battle of the arts involved the *trivium* against the *quadrivium*, and involved leading mathematicians of the day, like Galileo Galilei and Descartes, defending their discipline against attacks by Renaissance humanists, coming largely from within the schools of the Jesuits.

Recent discoveries in astronomy had precipitated this fight. Early on in the Renaissance, humanist poets and rhetoricians had never anticipated that reading ancient authors would one day spur an interest in ancient magic, physics, astrology, and astronomy, and that such interest would lead to Copernicus, discovery of the telescope, the rise of mathematics and the *quadrivium*, and transformation of the *trivium* into the *trivial*. None of this was part of Petrarch's dream.

Nonetheless, by the early part of the seventeenth century, the mathematical star was rising in the colleges and universities of the West, most of which had been recently established by the Jesuits as part of the counter-Reformation around a heavily humanist curriculum. As the ascendancy of mathematics occurred, mathematicians increasingly came under heated attack from other disciplines, including "teachers of philosophy." Attacks against mathematicians became especially sharp at one point at the famed Jesuit Collegio Romano. So sharp that renowned Galileo scholar William Wallace reports, "the distinguished Jesuit mathematician Father Christopher Clavius entered the dispute in the form of a 'disquisition for the Society of Jesus about the way in which the mathematical disciplines could be promoted in the schools of the Society.'"[46]

Wallace adds that, in the late 1580s, Clavius issued several "prescriptions," including "a warning about professors of philosophy who gave an improper interpretation to passages in Aristotle and in other philosophers." Clavius's warning says: "It will also contribute to this if the teachers of philosophy abstained from those questions which do not help in the understanding of natural things and very much detract from the authority of the mathematical disciplines in the eyes of the students, such as those in which they teach that mathematical sciences are not sciences, do not have demonstrations, abstract from being and the good, etc.; for experience teaches that these questions are a great hindrance to pupils and of no service to them; especially since teachers can hardly teach them without bringing these sciences into ridicule (which I do not just know from hearsay.)"[47]

When we take these attacks against the background of the pervasive influence of Renaissance humanism, the Renaissance humanists' fanciful tale about the origin and nature of philosophy, and the propensity of the Renaissance mind to view the world as a

---

[46] William Wallace, *Galileo and His Sources: The Heritage of the Collegio Romano* (Princeton, N.J.: Princeton University Press, 1984), 136–137.

[47] Wallace, *Galileo and His Sources: The Heritage of the Collegio Romano*, 137.

book, a new significance occurs to: (1) Galileo's famous quip in *The Assayer* that the book of nature "is written in the language of mathematics and the characters are triangles, circles and other geometrical figures" and (2) Descartes's pursuit of philosophy as a system of clear and distinct ideas. In both cases, these thinkers appear to be: (1) directly addressing Renaissance humanists and (2) calling into question the humanist claim to be the intermediaries between ordinary human beings and true philosophy and the universe.

Against this background, Descartes's dream of uncovering a new science of clear and distinct ideas buried in his mind was clearly a mathematician's response to the exaggerated claim of Renaissance humanists that philosophy is a hidden teaching transmitted historically by poets. In reaction to this assertion, Descartes replied that philosophy is no hidden teaching historically transmitted. It is a system of clear and distinct ideas clearly apprehensible to the exceptional individual possessed of the right method of self-reflection.

Descartes had thought that centuries of compounded bad learning habits caused by the wandering poetic imagination had buried this clear system of truth within Descartes's, and everyone else's, mind. All that was needed to overcome this situation was the right method to stabilize the wandering poetic imagination and make it subservient to pure, mathematical reason. Hence, only an exceptional individual, a single original thinker (what Renaissance humanists had called a *priscus theologus poeta*), a heroic person of secular, mathematical faith seeking mathematical understanding, could apprehend the pristine truth buried therein and restore it.[48]

No longer would mathematicians and teachers of the *quadrivium* be shackled by the excessive claims to authority made by teachers of the *trivium*. With Descartes, the 'Battle of the Arts' had taken a decisively new turn. Sir Isaac Newton and Jean-Jacques Rousseau, the other main leaders of the 'Age of Reason,' would react to this new turn and, in large part, account for transmission of the thought of Averroes and the Masters of the Arts of Paris to the freethinkers of the seventeenth and eighteenth centuries.

While many of Descartes's mathematical colleagues celebrated his method, Newton was somewhat displeased by the way Descartes had chosen to elevate mathematics above poetry. Newton did not subscribe to the Renaissance poets' claims to authority. But he accepted the Renaissance Hebraist account of philosophy's origin and nature. Descartes's view of philosophy's nature and origin undermined this account.

Descartes was no anti-Semite. Still, unwittingly his view of philosophy's nature and origin deflated the elevated cultural status of the Israelites that Renaissance humanists had ascribed to them. In Descartes's understanding of the nature and origin of philosophy,

---

[48] Wallace, *Galileo and His Sources: The Heritage of the Collegio Romano*, 27–34.

Chapter 5: Petrarch's Failed Project 145

the Jews play no special role, except, perhaps, negative. If we consider Descartes's view against the background of the Renaissance humanist account of philosophy's nature and origin, *implicit in his teaching* is that, by inculcating us with bad learning habits, for centuries, the Israelites and their followers had prevented us from reaching pure reason and from discovering the true system of science buried within our minds.

Whether Newton saw these implications in Descartes's view of philosophy I do not know. Recent scholarship, however, indicates Newton thought, that during his time, Western freethinkers had started to attack the status of Jewish learning. Newton maintained that some freethinkers intentionally sought to undermine Scriptural authority by deflating the status of Jewish learning and elevating the status of non-Jewish civilizations. Wittingly or unwittingly, Descartes's dream about the nature and origin of philosophy deconstructed the elevated position that Renaissance humanists tended to give to Jewish culture.[49] Apparently, some freethinkers were already capitalizing on this deconstruction.

Newton sought to protect Christianity against similar deconstruction and to fight the spread of idolatry in his day by using mathematics to demystify Scripture and the universe. He wanted to show that Judeo-Christian revelation is not superstitious. Indeed, it contains the scientific system of rational truth (modern

---

[49] Redpath, *Masquerade of the Dream Walkers: Prophetic Theology from the Cartesians to Hegel* (Amsterdam and Atlanta: Editions Rodopi, B.V., 1998), 13–16.

rationalism!) about the workings of the whole universe that God had originally revealed directly to Moses. *Moses, in short, had the clear and distinct idea of science as a system long before Descartes.* And it was contained in historical revelation, not in some innate idea buried in the mind.

Newton considered philosophy to be deflated theology, historical truth about God's operation in creation.[50] He looked upon the whole universe and its parts as a riddle, a secret, that he could read by applying pure thought to certain evidence, "certain mythic clues which God had left about the world to allow a sort of philosopher's treasure hunt to the esoteric brotherhood." Newton believed that a secret brotherhood had transmitted these truths about the nature of universe in an unbroken chain back to the original cryptic revelation in Babylonia.[51] He thought that, "throughout history, God continuously raised up prophets to lead his people back to the original truth revealed to the first followers of Jesus."[52] He believed he was one of these prophets, a Magi "de-

---

[50] Redpath, *Wisdom's Odyssey*, 15–16 See, also, Frank E. Manuel, *Isaac Newton, Historian* (Cambridge, Mass.: Harvard University Press, 1979), 89–121, 139–168.

[51] John Maynard Keynes, "Newton the Man," in *Newton*, ed. I. Bernard Cohen and Richard S. Westfall (New York and London: W. W. Norton and Company, Inc., 1995), 315.

[52] Redpath, *Masquerade of the Dream Walkers: Prophetic Theology from the Cartesians to Hegel*, 13. See, also, Redpath, *Wisdom's Odyssey from Philosophy to Transcendental Sophistry*, 133–145.

Chapter 5: Petrarch's Failed Project   147

scended from a long line of scientific prophets who had anticipated his discoveries in a prefigured and oracular fashion."[53] Apparently, he saw his birth on 25 December 1642 as a sign of his special relation to the Magi.

At the time that Marsilio Ficino's Platonic Academy started to exert an influence at Cambridge University through individuals like Ralph Cudworth and Henry More, Newton was Lucasian Professor of Mathematics at Trinity College.[54] He was also an Arian.[55] As an Arian at Trinity College, of Cambridge University, Newton had a special problem. Historically, Arianism was a Christian heresy that denied the divinity of Jesus. Public knowledge of his theological views could have cost him his job. Hence, in his public life, he adopted the posture of the Latin Averroists before him, adherence to a standard of double truth. He said one thing in public that he contradicted in private.

Under More's influence, Newton also accepted the Renaissance humanist apocryphal definition of philosophy as a hidden body of knowledge. He thought this was a magical philosophy, a doctrine about the workings of the universe, and a simple moral code, an original monotheistic Christian religion that God had

---

[53] Redpath, *Masquerade of the Dream Walkers: Prophetic Theology from the Cartesians to Hegel*, 20.

[54] Redpath, *Masquerade of the Dream Walkers: Prophetic Theology from the Cartesians to Hegel*, 13.

[55] Redpath, *Masquerade of the Dream Walkers: Prophetic Theology from the Cartesians to Hegel*, 20. See, also, Cohen and Westfall, *Newton*, 327–328, and Westfall, "Newton and Christianity," in *Newton*, 368.

given to human beings when He first created religion. Newton claimed that God had originally revealed this magical philosophy to Moses. Later it became obscured, and was partly rediscovered by some ancient sages.

In a fashion similar to Averroes and to many Renaissance humanists, Newton believed that Scripture hides a true teaching, philosophy, or science. But, according to Newton, this teaching is about the history of creation, the original Christian religion, not a mystical and esoteric moral or metaphysical system. And, in standard Renaissance humanist fashion, he maintained that the educational deficiency of their audience had caused Moses and other Biblical authors to describe this creation history poetically, to make it comprehensible.[56]

Rousseau is the other major thinker of the Age of Reason coming after Descartes whose reaction to him plays a crucial role in transmitting an Averroistic mindset from the Masters of the Arts of Paris to Enlightenment freethinkers. Rousseau did this by substantially changing Descartes's dream into the Enlightenment spirit by giving what I call an 'evolutionary-Heraclitean twist' to the Renaissance humanist notion of philosophy's nature and history. To achieve this change, Rousseau: (1) reduced matter to spirit and (2) conceived Descartes's scientific system of clear and distinct ideas spiritually and historically to emerge, in an Averroistic

---

[56] Redpath, *Masquerade of the Dream Walkers: Prophetic Theology from the Cartesians to Hegel*, 13–35.

Chapter 5: Petrarch's Failed Project   149

mental trinity, through the ideas of tolerance, progress, and the voice of conscience, from prior obscure ideas.[57]

Rousseau realized that the success of Descartes's dream to join all our ideas into a unified scientific system depended upon overcoming a weakness in Descartes's 'philosophy.' Descartes had attempted to remove magic and spiritualism from the scientific universe by maintaining that only two substances exist, mind and matter, and that they cannot communicate.

The reason for this is that matter is totally inactive, while spirit is the only thing that acts. He had a problem with this view, upon which he founded his claim to have discovered the scientific system of clear and distinct ideas. In the real world, matter and mind communicate. Descartes could not explain this communication between the substances of mind, or spirit, and matter. Rousseau resigned to overcome this failure by accepting a position that Descartes had rejected: "modern philosophy's principles are essentially dualistic, animistic, and obscure."[58]

Hence, Rousseau maintained that "only spirits are substances." He thought that only spirits exist and even "apparently inanimate beings, like stones, are animate." They are sensitive, but devoid of

---

[57] Redpath, *Masquerade of the Dream Walkers: Prophetic Theology from the Cartesians to Hegel*, 80–99.

[58] Redpath, *Masquerade of the Dream Walkers: Prophetic Theology from the Cartesians to Hegel*, 91. See, also, Jean-Jacques Rousseau, *Émile or On Education*, trans. Allan Bloom, New York: Basic Books, Inc., Publishers, 1979), 273–275.

sensations, much as an angel would be intellective, but not intellectual, if it were a pure intellect empty of ideas.[59]

While Rousseau accepted Descartes's claim that science is a system of clear and distinct ideas, he rejected Descartes's contention that God had given us this system simultaneously whole in a multitude of clear and distinct ideas buried in our mind, and Newton's view that God had given this in immediate revelation to Moses. Instead, Rousseau maintained that God has intended this system of science to emerge from the human race through progressive self-development (what we, today, call 'progress'). And, in this process, God intends humanity's true teacher to be a person of inspired, or enlightened, faith, the singular person of strong feeling who has only nature as a teacher.[60]

In his famous work, *Émile*, Rousseau articulates in detail nature's education of humanity's true teacher, rare and abstract man, "a child of Enlightenment and pure reason." Emile is this child: the book of nature, a *tabula rasa* [a blank slate] of pure feeling and spirit. Emile thus symbolizes the Renaissance definition of hidden philosophy prior to becoming conscious of itself: the conflation of poetic imagination, prophecy, and natural revelation, impelled by the infallible, transcendent voice of conscience, duty, to *emerge out of itself*, reveal itself, and become the science of clear and distinct

---

[59] Redpath, *Masquerade of the Dream Walkers: Prophetic Theology from the Cartesians to Hegel*, 92. See, also, Rousseau, *Émile*, 285–287.

[60] Redpath, *Masquerade of the Dream Walkers: Prophetic Theology from the Cartesians to Hegel*, 72–73. See, also, Rousseau, *Émile*, 285–287.

Chapter 5: Petrarch's Failed Project

ideas. Hence, Rousseau tells us, "Emile can only accept as true what is self-persuasive according to his historical order of growth."[61]

Rousseau maintains that conscience is a way of speaking: an oracle, or *voice*, produced as a result of a system of human emotions (sensations of the self as a body) feeling themselves together, emerging, into a system of other, self-disclosed, individual emotions (the idea of self as spirit). Union of these two systems of emotion generates the voice we call 'conscience': a voice that moves us to transport ourselves from one system into another, from a child of mechanical instinct to a moral agent, to a civic being. For Rousseau, the voice of conscience is God's voice, free speech, an act of disclosure whereby the system of nature transports itself (human nature), according to an Averroistic mental trinity, beyond a more primitive mechanical system to a social and, finally, political system. Conscience does this by changing the way we talk (just as a male's voice changes as he enters adolescence) as we move from the lower stage to the higher.

At the mechanical stage of human instinct, which corresponds to Averroes's totally imaginative and emotional level of the ordinary believer, persuaded only by oratorical arguments, Rousseau thinks that God's voice (conscience) speaks through the mechanical voice of human instinct, human nature viewed as a dumb animal, or machine. At the moral stage of educational development,

---

[61] Redpath, *Masquerade of the Dream Walkers: Prophetic Theology from the Cartesians to Hegel*, 93. See, also, Rousseau, *Émile*, 285–287.

which corresponds to Averroes's second stage of symbolic mind of the logician and theologian, God's voice still speaks through the Book of Nature.

But the Book of Nature is humanity having emerged toward the first, primitive stage of Enlightenment reason, not the book of mechanical human instinct. At this point, the system of enlightened ideas enables God for the first time in human history, to utter his voice, and make it heard by the human spirit, not just by the body. That is, human beings get a taste of spirit, of freedom!

According to Rousseau, 'conscience' cannot exist prior to the existence of knowledge and reason, the civic stage of complete Enlightenment. This corresponds to Averroes's most true and abstract mind of the philosopher, which apprehends, learns, and teaches truth in an absolute sense in its hidden, interior meaning, through scientific demonstration. Before humanity reaches this stage, Rousseau holds that what we call 'conscience' is a primitive, mechanical-like groping toward the human good. Only the enlightened system of ideas can make conscience emerge because non-enlightened ideas (1) are obscure and indistinct and (2) cannot produce audible sound. Rousseau maintains that they generate the counterfeit noise of fanatics. Hence, prior to the Enlightenment, conscience had no voice.

After Rousseau, using Rousseau's model, freethinkers like Gotthold Ephraim Lessing, Immanuel Kant, and Georg Wilhelm Friedrich Hegel will further transform Descartes's dream of a scientific system into an Enlightened spiritualism. They will do this by uniting the spirit of Averroes and the popular Renaissance humanist apocryphal definition of philosophy already present in Newton and Rousseau. Thus, the spirit of Averroes remains alive and well in the twentieth century, in the progeny of Kant and Hegel.

In my opinion, the future of our civilization depends upon our recognizing this fact. It also depends upon recognizing that this spirit is not philosophical. It is poetic, sophistic, and spiritualistic. Failure to recognize this fact violates two laws of philosophical experience: *Things tend to act according to their natures* and *Philosophy always buries its undertakers.* This is true whether these undertakers be poets, rhetoricians, logicians, great religions, or civilizations. We ignore this law at our peril!

www.ingramcontent.com/pod-product-compliance
Lightning Source LLC
LaVergne TN
LVHW051837080426
835512LV00018B/2919